SUBVERSION AND SUBSIDY

THE FRENCH LIST

SUBVERSION AND SUBSIDY

contemporary art and aesthetics

RAINER ROCHLITZ

TRANSLATED BY DAFYDD ROBERTS

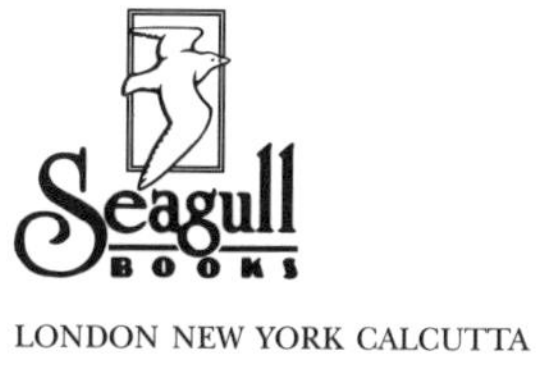

LONDON NEW YORK CALCUTTA

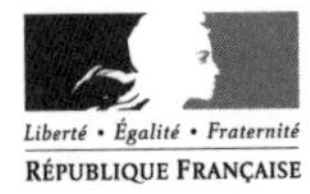

Liberté • Égalité • Fraternité
RÉPUBLIQUE FRANÇAISE

Publication of this book is supported by the French Ministry
of Foreign Affairs as part of the Burgess Programme run by
the Cultural Department of the French Embassy in London.

Seagull Books

Editorial offices:

1st Floor, Angel Court, 81 St Clements Street
Oxford OX4 1AW, UK

1 Washington Square Village, Apt 1U
New York, NY 10012, USA

26 Circus Avenue, Calcutta 700 017, India

© Editions GALLIMARD, Paris, 1994

English translation © Dafydd Roberts 2008
First published in English by Seagull Books, 2008

ISBN-13   978 1 9054 2 270 8 (HB)
ISBN-13   978 1 9054 2 271 5 (PB)

Jacket design by Sunandini Banerjee using a photograph by Naveen Kishore.

British Library Cataloguing-in-Publication Data
A catalogue record for this book is available
from the British Library

Typeset by Seagull Books, Calcutta, India
Printed and bound in the United Kingdom by Biddles Lyd, King's Lynn

To G., the perplexed artist

CONTENTS

1

In art, as for society more generally, it is harder to define a new and unprecedented situation than to tack on a 'post-' to mark the passing of a period or the obsolescence of a conceptual apparatus become familiar and convenient. Contrary to the belief of certain intellectual currents of the seventies and eighties, modernity isn't a fashion that can by jettisoned by changing style or giving up certain dogmatic rigours. The collapse of certainty being as liable to induce intoxication as its advent, the deflation of today—still marked, in the negative, by the absolutes that have departed—already sometimes takes itself for a new certainty. The consequence of the irrevocable decline of pre-modern traditions and of the political and economic instability of industrial societies, the problems however persist, or return in other guises, preventing any going back to the past; but the nature of conceivable responses and solutions has changed.

The arts have seen the emergence of no convincing work capable of outflanking the moderns, whose tradition is not in any case 'traditionalist'. Inherited genres once allowed artists to concentrate above all on technical problems. With the passage of time, innovation was, one might say, an inevitable by-product. Since Duchamp, Joyce and Cage, the arts have been faced with the choice of either offering variations on traditional models, as an adornment to life, or reinventing art as the object of an undivided attention, useless as decoration, divertissement or background. Hence the dissolution of the alliance between decoration and ambitious artistic research, which Matisse was the last to reconcile and which design, today, has not succeeded in reuniting.

To this significant rupture, masked by the mass culture that has developed around contemporary art as if it were still an adjunct to style, must be added its management by the public authorities. Ignored as a deliberate insult to the established order during the first half of the twentieth century, contemporary art has been reclaimed for the national heritage and granted a triumphal entry into the public galleries. This integration of subversive art has a number of features in common with the pacification of social conflict through the welfare state. Whatever their shortcomings, the subsidies accorded to the arts at the municipal, regional and national levels are the equivalent of the social gains of the post-war period, sharing the same fluctuating destiny. Contemporary society feels obliged to display open-mindedness, understanding and tolerance towards practices that through modernist and avant-gardist experiment have learnt how to put their finger on the most vulnerable and contestable aspects of social reality, revealing what in our private and public lives we would rather not look at directly.

Aesthetic theory, most often a purely academic exercise, has thus found itself obliged to enter an arena that goes beyond its own exclusive competence. Traditionally, the art-lover was not concerned with the significance and status of art as a human activity. Today, however, the upheaval in the 'spheres of value' has led to a questioning of the social role and intrinsic meaning of an activity organized and subsidized by the authorities that promises an indefinable pleasure yet obstinately refuses it. The difficulty is to understand why government and private investors support a culture that by definition can come to no peace with its patrons nor with the public in general—a situation that has disoriented criticism and undermined the status of art in the eyes of the public. It is unlike that which obtained in the pre-modern period, when art was largely in the service of Church or Court, or the modern, where it had to survive in the face of a hostile market and a lack of institutional support.

2

A distinction has to be drawn, then, between the internal structure and problematic of art and the impact of the new institutional context, identifying first of all the necessity intrinsic to art, its own distinctive logic or rationality.

In his theory of the rationalization of Western societies, Max Weber located the rationality of art only in the rational organization of its techniques and its modes of institutionalization, ignoring the inner logic of the individual work. In art too, for him, rationality meant calculation and rational economy of means to achieve a given end. He never envisaged the possibility of a logic of the artwork itself, a reconstruction of its own claim to success and of the criteria by which it is to be judged.

For Theodor Adorno, 'aesthetic rationality' represented—by virtue of a kind of 'Pascal's vase' mechanism—the rationality expelled by the instrumental spirit of society: that of a *mimesis* in sympathy with nature. This is why the logic of the artwork had always to signify something other than itself: a criticism of, or compensation for, what was missing in the social.

Aesthetics was a way of continuing by other means the social theory of Marx and Weber. Yet while it is true that the concerns of a work of art are not those of another world than this, it is wrong to attribute to art in its diversity the role abandoned by the working class as the initiator of social subversion.

In reconsidering Weber's thought so as to establish the basis for a critical theory of society, Jürgen Habermas did not attempt to reconstruct the 'aesthetic rationality' that Adorno had made too much of; rather, he developed, in relation to moral and legal questions, a model of differential rationalization no more than adumbrated in Weber, a model not without consequences for aesthetics. In modern society, Weber had said, art is constituted as a 'universe of distinctive, autonomous, conscious values',[1] such that it is capable of developing 'in accordance with its own laws'.[2] But rather than pursuing this idea of a specifically artistic type of rationality, Weber went on to consider only the progress of technique, which precisely cannot be identified with progress in art itself, and the social role of this rationalized sphere, which is precisely minimal.

From the point of view of a theory of argumentation, aesthetic rationalization would seem to be grounded in the 'critical capacity for assessing value', which, like the cognitive capacity to register facts or the moral capacity to refer to norms, is linked to a basic function of everyday discourse; in other words, art would be a provider of values through which

---

1 Max Weber, 'Religious Rejections of the World and their Directions' in H. H. Gerth and C. Wright Mills (eds), *From Max Weber: Essays in Sociology* (New York: Oxford University Press, 1958), cited in Jürgen Habermas, *The Theory of Communicative Action*, VOL. 1, *Reason and the Rationalization of Society*, trans. Thomas McCarthy (Cambridge: Polity Press, 1991), p. 160. [Translation modified to accord with the French.]

2 Habermas, *Theory of Communicative Action*, p. 160. [Translation modified.]

we express our subjective preferences.[3] But these values are in fact only the secondary by-products of an 'aesthetic rationality' deployed in the creation and appreciation of works of art themselves according to criteria of artistic success.

Unlike the evaluative conception, the idea of art as a means of 'access to the world'[4] takes up the Weberian notion of the 'non-quotidian' nature of the aesthetic sphere, in this respect analogous to the religious and the erotic. As a mere possibility, such an opening must prove itself by casting new light on the everyday. Furthermore, the power of affording access to the world is not exclusive to art: philosophy; religion and the human sciences also have it. It is independent of the artistic quality of the work, so that the fact of presenting a new perspective on the world is neither the sole nor a sufficient aesthetic criterion.

3

Politically, the non-quotidian in Weber is associated with personal charisma, based on magical power and incapable of stable institutionalization.[5] Modern rationalization and desacralization confine the religious, artistic

---

3 Habermas thus reproaches Nietzsche for not having recognized 'as a moment of reason the critical capacity for assessing value that was sharpened through dealing with modern art—a moment that is still at least procedurally connected with objectifying knowledge and moral insight in the processes of providing argumentative grounds' (see Jürgen Habermas, *The Philosophical Discourse of Modernity*, trans. Frederick Lawrence, Cambridge: Polity Press, 1987, p. 960).

4 Habermas, *Theory of Communicative Action*, p. 69.

5 Max Weber, *Economy and Society: An Outline of Interpretive Sociology*, ed. Guenther Roth and Claus Wittich (Berkeley: University of California Press, 1978), p. 1111ff.

and erotic non-quotidian to the domain of subjective experience, without direct purchase on the cognitive and normative orders, which follow another logic. Such is the dominant vision of modernity. In Georges Bataille, on the other hand, religion as 'inner experience', eroticism, art, literature and poetry are the subject of one single study concerned with 'excess energy, translated into the effervescence of life'[6] or 'nonproductive expenditure'.[7] Like the great aesthetic theorists informed by early-twentieth-century sociology—Simmel, Lukács, Bloch, Benjamin and Adorno—Bataille too starts with Weber, only to invert his conclusions: 'it is certain that the revolution effected by the Reformation has, as Weber saw, a profound significance: It marked the passage to a new form of economy. Referring back to the spirit of the great reformers, one can even say that by accepting the extreme consequences of a demand for religious purity, it destroyed the sacred world, the world of nonproductive consumption, and handed the earth over to the men of production, to the bourgeois.'[8] For Bataille, as for the Benjamin of the *Origins of German Tragic Drama,* the destruction of the sacred, far from being definitive, is no more than a subjective appearance: 'It can be said, finally, that starting from then *things* dominated man, in so far as he lived for enterprise and less and less in the present time. But domination is never total, and in a deep sense it is only a comedy: It never deceives more than partly, while in the propitious darkness a new truth turns stormy.'[9] In the same way, Walter Benjamin sees announced in baroque allegory an inversion of sacralization and the

---

6 Georges Bataille, *The Accursed Share: An Essay on General Economy,* VOL. 1, trans. Robert Hurley (New York: Zone Books, 1991), p. 10.

7 Ibid., p. 12.

8 Ibid., p. 127.

9 Ibid., p. 133.

triumph of subjectivity in the modern world. The hell of modernity is only a subjective illusion, and 'in the image that allegory gives of the world the subjective perspective is . . . totally included in the economy of the whole',[10] a theological economy that remains intact despite all the social changes wrought by modernity.

These philosophers thus attempt to relativize the logics of modern science and law in the name of an aesthetic vision supposed to maintain the ascendancy of the sacred. In the face of such a resacralization of the world—one that does not recognize that modern societies, Protestant or not, have done away with the sacred foundation of social life—it is easy for positivism to insist that in modern society the work of art no longer has any normative value, and answers only to the subjective criterion of pleasure. And it is indeed true that nothing obliges us to subscribe to the visions offered by works of art, and that deprived of their sacred functions they now answer to profane criteria.

All attempts to return to art the cultic and cultural authority it once enjoyed have failed. More recently, every social sphere has been overtaken by a hedonistic aestheticization, from shop-windows and packaging to advertising and the media, to the office, sports and politics. Between a sacred desperately resuscitated and such generalized hedonism, is there still a place, necessarily within art itself, for a logic profane yet independent of the pleasure principle, demanding yet without any pretension to dogmatic authority, free of any social obligation yet susceptible of rigorous critique?

---

10 Walter Benjamin, *The Origins of German Tragic Drama*, trans. John Osborne (London: New Left Books, 1977), p. 234.

4

Such then is the paradox of aesthetic argumentation, to be concerned with a rational necessity that has no basis in quotidian discourse and behaviour and whose rationality is founded upon an openness to the sphere of art, an openness that cannot however be demanded of anyone. No one is obliged to create a remarkable work, or to devote time and attention to it; but once we do attend, we are engaged by its logic, judging it good, admiring or appreciating it, or bad, as if any imperfection were a fault comparable to an untruth or a moral failing, so that the self-critical artist bears a weighty responsibility and finds him/herself liable to a quasi-excommunication by criticism.

This is another aspect of the fundamental paradox of artistic 'beauty': unlike natural beauty, which claims nothing, the work of art puts forward the claim to be beautiful, successful and absolutely relevant—to everyone, that is to say, rather than to one person or to a few friends, like the work of the amateur. Otherwise, as Kant correctly insists, one would be wrong to use the word beautiful, which implies an intersubjective validity. However, there are few if any works that evoke not only the expert admiration of the critics but also the spontaneous assent of all. Every work of art irreducibly arises from a partial point of view on the world in which only a part of the public happily discovers a possible meaning of life. Whether a work is a success or a failure can be rationally justified; whether it speaks to me depends on another kind of discourse. This kind of legitimate preference escapes rationality in the strict sense, involving reasons that bind no one and which each individual may invoke in support of their own evaluations and their own personal taste.

Reflection on contemporary art comes to reveal what is an ensemble of structural constraints. At the first level, there is the *situation* created by the emancipation of art, more particularly since the early twentieth century, characterized by an apparently limitless freedom, gained since the days of the early avant-gardes. Criticism, however, has had difficulty in following the development of art beyond the reach of any established definition. Having had to abandon all traditional criteria, successively identified as prejudices and put into question by artists, it takes refuge today either in an attitude of rejection, in the expectation of a 'return to order', or in a blind and unquestioning solidarity with whatever at any time passes for 'important', or again in an anaesthetized neutrality, indifferent to contemporary art and concerned only to commit as few faux pas as possible. It is in this context that there have emerged voices, some timid and worried about notions of quality, others authoritarian and ready with censure, that call for the re-establishment of something like criteria.

At a second level, aesthetic judgement attempts to arm itself in the face of the new situation, constructing the elements of an 'aesthetic logic' or the central concepts with which to *argue* about works of art. If today a beginning has been made on the delineation of such a logic, it could not have been as clearly conceived without the experience of the art of the twentieth century, which precisely gave the lie to the constitutive prejudices of the most prudent of earlier aesthetics. It is opposed at the same time to those discourses that claim that aesthetics no longer has anything to say about contemporary works, or, going even further, that any rational discourse is defeated by the structure of the image.

It is not however enough to have criteria of what is art and of what counts towards its quality. For at the last stage, the *institutional and political* context of contemporary art tends to neutralize these criteria. Unlike in pre-modern periods, which subjected artists to the control of their patrons, and unlike too the modern period, which made the emancipated and subversive artist the victim of a generally obtuse society, the contemporary period endeavours to institutionalize revolt, subsidizing subversion. This society that claims to have laid social conflicts to rest also claims to accept the systematic anti-conformism of the emancipated arts. It must be required to prove that it has not opened its temples to an insubordinate art only in order to neutralize its explosive force.

Contemporary art, for its part, has to assume its two contradictory inheritances: that of a sovereignty dearly bought by a heroic modern art, virtually independent of any institution, and that of a new dependence on public and private institutions, more or less generous depending on the economic conjuncture, and which, following in the footsteps of the Vatican, whose museums have exhibited the anti-papist paintings of Francis Bacon, are greedy even for insulting novelties, happy to boast of the artist's subversion and to subsidize the 'hostile' culture that contemporary society offers itself as a little luxury.

PART ONE **}** **situation**

the conquest and abdication of aesthetic sovereignty: breaks in the modernist logic

Even before coming up against the requirements of the institutions, there is another type of constraint that operates within creative activity itself. Independently of the narrow notion of 'avant-garde', the history of the arts has an irreversibility, a directionality deriving from the accumulation of knowledge that no artist can ignore with impunity. But this knowledge can be handled in different ways, and avant-gardism is not the only option.

In contemporary art, the real break in the modernist logic seems to be marked by the emergence of German and American Neo-Expressionism (Baselitz, Immendorf, Penck, Kiefer, Schnabel) and the Italian Transavanguardia (Chia, Paladino, Cucchi, Clemente). Looking at 'the new slurried canvases, immense and bombastic, puerile and portentous, shallow and brash', Arthur C. Danto said to himself, 'This was not the way things were supposed to go next.' This art was contrary to the whole logic that Danto had constructed on the basis of the American art of the previous decades. It seemed to him that 'art must after all have an ordered history, a way in which things have to go rather than some other way. Art history must have an internal structure and even a kind of necessity.'[1] This was why Danto was certain that 'art does not have that kind of future.'[2] And given this, he could have expected the emergence of a type of contemporary art that would indeed accord with the 'necessity' he saw, consigning Neo-Expressionism to a conformist limbo that had nothing to do with the 'history of art'. Yet he preferred to hold, Hegel-like, that the 'necessary' history of art had come to an end, and that Neo-Expressionism was the proof: 'We have entered a period of post-historical art, where the need for constant self-revolutionization of art is now past . . . We are entering a more stable, more happy period of artistic endeavour where the basic needs to which art has always been responsive may again be met.'[3]

Rather than question his own diagnosis, according to which Warhol's *Brillo Boxes*—a recreation of the packaging—represented the *nec plus ultra* of the history of art, the point 'when it is known what art is and means',[4] Danto prefers to exclude Neo-Expressionism from the history of art, counting it among the distractions of post-history. But why then should he question its historical legitimacy? Dissatisfied at not having found in it the 'necessity' he believed he discerned in the history of modern art, Danto comes to a judgement of taste and a judgement of philosophy. But these two judgements are contradictory: the philosopher should in principle accept what his judgement of taste rejects.

Rejecting Danto's analysis and claiming that 'history continues', Catherine Millet names a number of contemporary artists whom she iden-

---

1 Arthur C. Danto, *The Philosophical Disenfranchisement of Art* (New York: Columbia University Press, 1986), p. xiv.

2 Ibid., p. xiii.

3 Ibid., p. xv.

4 Ibid., p. 111.

tifies as opposed to 'eclecticism and culture-zapping': Immendorf, Jacquet, Salle, Art & Language.[5] This is a list that can itself hardly escape the accusation of eclecticism, if in another sense: why Immendorf rather than Polke or Baselitz, why Jacquet rather than Garouste? And why all these *and* Art & Language? All that such a personal selection can prove is that there still exists an 'ambitious' art that 'wrests us for a moment from the flux' of culture-zapping,[6] but which does not at all allow the identification of any directionality; the fact that 'history continues' does not prove that Danto is wrong and that these are any more than simple 'post-historical' exercises.

Donald Judd's analysis sets aside from the start the 'judgement of taste' that he sees as irrelevant to contemporary art. What is important for him is the criterion of 'newness', which Neo-Expressionism fails to satisfy:

> Expressionism is not an important idea in the art of this century, since it is the weakest attempt to deal with the disintegration of traditional representation, in fact even a reactionary one, being just a distortion of the picture. . . .
>
> . . . Many artists recently are similar to Baselitz . . . Neither is the present fashion a novelty; there has been a new fashion biannually for 15 years. The present characteristics in common are the constant derivation, usually blown-up, and the crassness of the execution. Schnabel is better than Baselitz but this work is derivative from 'Abstract Expressionism' and inferior to a hundred artists of 25 years ago, some good and many still alive. There's a little *art brut* and primitivism, neither new, for innovation.

---

5 Catherine Millet, 'Ce n'est qu'un début, l'art continue', *Art Press*, special issue, *L'histoire continue* (1992), p. 16.

6 Ibid.

Schnabel and his audience are ignorant of the past situation as history, which leads to worse, a cultural ignorance in their acceptance of the stale eclecticism. Chia is rehashing academic mythology, including Picasso's waltzing Hellenistic figures, bad when Picasso did them and decadent in the first place. A great deal of expensive oil paint makes an impasto, another guaranteed symbol, that is colorless, leaden and boring. Such work has always been around; only its size is new, derivative, many years later, from Newman, Pollock and the others. The same with Clemente. There's nothing new in the affected primitivism, only that it's blown-up. The kitsch classicism of Garouste is that of a Sunday painter of 30 years ago in the Washington Square Outdoor Show. Finally, the worst paintings, historical only in regard to [19]30s magazine illustration, but mentionable as the ultimate in vapidity, hopefully, are those of David Salle.[7]

Forgetting the entirely analogous unwelcome he was offered by Clement Greenberg and Michael Fried in the sixties, in the name of a polemical concept of regressive 'theatricality', Judd, more committed than Danto, does not resign himself to accepting a 'post-historical' artistic situation. Judd establishes a connection between what he sees as the aesthetic regression of Neo-Expressionism and the political and moral regression that accompanies the 'return to painting':

The nationalism in some of the German work is very reactionary, and is also kitsch, and should not be dis-

---

7 Donald Judd, 'A long discussion not about master-pieces but about why there are so few of them: Part I', *Art in America* 72/8 (September 1984), p. 13.

missed as just one more artist's fancy . . . One of the worst paintings I've ever seen in all respects is one by Anselm Kiefer in the Venice Biennale of 1980. The busts of German cultural heroes were lined around a room. Everything was badly painted on purpose and colored the brown children get when they mix all the colors together. Perhaps it's a parody of nationalism but I think not. If not, the painting is a support for the most destructive force in the world, an obsolescent force like that of the Empires of the First War, and similarly set to explode as it collapses.[8]

It is true that Georg Baselitz lays provocative claim to a 'nationalism',[9] in the sense of an insistence on the specificity of different cultural traditions which he opposes to the 'boring internationalism' of the Americans. His series *Ciao America* complements *1945*, itself an allusion to a year that the artist, who remained in East Germany until 1958, did not experience as a liberation.[10] In Baselitz, the 'return to painting' comes increasingly to stand for an aesthetic anti-Americanism and for experiences of mourning and memory that reject any objective assessment in grasping German history from within Germany's responsibility. This rebel, the apolitical heir of 'degenerate painting', an artist who in 1963 saw his paintings seized in West Germany on account of their 'obscenity', has come to occupy an almost unparalleled position in the art market. Despite his ambiguities,

---

8 Ibid.

9 Georg Baselitz, 'Interview avec Démosthène Davettas', *Art Press* 123 (March 1988), p. 12: 'It's true that German artists are nationalist—something that I find perfectly normal—and are hard to fit into the international framework.'

10 Georg Baselitz, 'Entretien avec Dieter Koepplin', *Art Press* 159 (June 1991), p. 19. Saxony was in fact 'liberated' by the Red Army.

the paintings resist ideological interpretation. His selective and ambivalent labour of memory, an endeavour to bridge the historical discontinuity by turning back from Abstract Expressionist to expressionist colour, succeeded in recovering possibilities that Minimal and Conceptual Art seemed to have rendered obsolete. He encouraged other painters to ignore the taboos laid down by the neo-avant-gardes which, in the hermeticism they imposed, ended up by depriving art of all critical or suggestive power. Indeed, rather than evidencing the 'end of the history of art' as Danto argued, contemporary art testifies to the loss of any model, to the extent that criticism finds itself obliged to examine each work on its own merits.

Having defended as exemplary the paradigms instantiated in the 'specific objects' and the *Brillo Boxes,* Judd and Danto could not accommodate the idea of a 'return to painting'. The critique of ideological regression is here based on an interpretation of the history of art as an irreversible process, such that the historical inscription of a work of art is decisive for the aesthetic quality to be attributed to it. In the same way, Benjamin Buchloh speaks of a return to figuration 'contrary to any aesthetic logic'[11] and Thierry de Duve of a 'return to painting which . . . disavows the precedent of the readymade'.[12] Implicitly, the latter conceives of *another* return to painting that does not: one that deliberately sets out to combat the photographic reproduction whose ascendancy over the visual image is one of the major features of our age. This is why Gerhard Richter and Robert Ryman are accorded canonical status by both Buchloh and de Duve.[13]

---

11 Benjamin Buchloh, essay in *Gerhard Richter* catalogue raisonné and exhibition catalogue, 3 VOLS (Bonn: Kunst-und Ausstellungshalle der Bundesrepublik Deutschland; Paris: Paris-musées, 1993); VOL. 2 (French version), *Essais*, p. 50.

12 Thierry de Duve, 'The Readymade and the Tube of Paint', *Artforum* 24/9 (May 1986), p. 111.

In one sense, the irreversibility of history means that certain advances cannot be left out of account. In another, it implies the duty to resolve the aporias the pioneers came up against:

> The sometimes seemingly irresoluble schism that Duchamp introduced into art, between the pure voluntarism of the aesthetic decree on the one hand and the universe of the unchangeable object on the other, found a solution—as in the work of other artists of the same period—in a new dialectic in Richter's work.[14]

These are two powerful constraints, in consequence of which no one may claim the title of contemporary artist without finding a response to the technical challenges of the image in the age of its mechanical reproducibility or without seeking a way through the problems inherited from earlier generations of artists. Some young artists define their goal by situating their project in relation to the 'debate' among recognized artists: by variation on the theme of the table introduced by Joseph Kosuth, of Warhol or Judd's 'box', etc. The art of today seems obliged, one way or another, to follow on from the 'avant-garde tradition'.[15] But what could a

---

13 Thierry de Duve, 'The Monochrome and the Blank Canvas' in Serge Guilbault (ed.), *Reconstructing Modernism: Art in New York, Paris, and Montreal 1945–1964* (Cambridge, MA: MIT Press, 1990), p. 299: 'Two of the greatest living painters, Robert Ryman and Gerhard Richter, are great precisely because they have acknowledged the readymade in their work while withstanding comparison with Manet.'

14 Buchloh, *Gerhard Richter* catalogue, VOL. 2, p. 75.

15 According to de Duve, neo-conservatives and postmodernists agree in 'deny[ing] that the avant-garde has been a tradition in the full sense of the word, that the works of the avant-garde are handed on, like those of the past, as examples to be emulated. They have confused works with ideologies' (Thierry de Duve, *Résonances du readymade: Duchamp entre avant-garde et tradition*, Nîmes: Jacqueline Chambon, 1989, p. 180).

'tradition' of breaking away from tradition mean? The reclamation of this concept for the avant-gardes either comes down to claiming a knowledge of the history of art in which one inscribes oneself in the very act of changing it or is a mere sophistry that serves to claim for the avant-gardes an 'authenticity' that they deny to the 'craft' tradition itself. It is difficult to deny a certain 'traditionalist' aspect to the 'return' to the painter's craft; to claim today the legitimacy of tradition for the avant-gardes because *they too* have been passed on—located in museums and still serving as exemplars—is to situate their posterity within the museum context, a context from which they had sought to escape.

The idea that the legitimacy of a work is related to its following on from the problems of its predecessors in no way implies an 'aesthetic judgement' in the Kantian sense, a judgement that 'founds, but does not justify a feeling',[16] in other words, it implies no subjective appreciation of the beauty or success of a work. These distinct expectations, to which may be added that of seeing the work respond to a paradigmatic experience of its age, remain to be articulated. One can say, provisionally, that a work that seeks, 'with eyes closed', to attain to beauty by ignoring both the technical problems of its predecessors and the bitter experience of the age, condemns itself to impotence.

But the distinction between an 'objective' registration of technical data and a 'subjective' aesthetic perception is itself problematic. This is shown, amongst others, by an observation by the two conceptual artists Michael Baldwin and Mel Ramsden, who—unlike their friend Kosuth—returned to painting:

---

16 Ibid., p. 187. See also Thierry de Duve, *Essais datés 1, 1974–1986* (Paris: Éditions de la Différence, 1987), pp. 128ff.

> When we did the *Portraits of V. I. Lenin in the Style of Jackson Pollock* we did about nine paintings and we discovered that some were 'better' than others. There had to be a reason for that. It rather sneaked up on us that this was connected with making the things rather than thinking them up. The actual practice of working on a painting has certain sorts of demands.[17]

This question of a quality that is neither purely subjective but having to do with 'reasons', nor purely objective and deducible from facts or concepts, still says nothing about the quality of the work as such, independently of the judgement of its creators. Their recourse to 'painterly daubs' for conceptual purposes is problematic, satisfying from neither the conceptual not the painterly point of view; and their 'conceptual' intentions, subversive of the institutions of painting and museum, can seem pointless when they are inevitably exhibited in the latter. Their question in any event put these artists in 'an uncomfortable situation, aware that this interminable modernity ha[d] not in the end disappeared'.[18]

stages of autonomy

The autonomy of art was won over many centuries and, as is witnessed by the periodic return of bans or threats against certain artists, is never definitively achieved. Since its conquest, it has been undermined by the very

---

17 David Batchelor, 'Art & Language: What Painting Means. Interviews with Michael Baldwin and Mel Ramsden', *Art Press* 185 (November 1993), p. E3.

18 From the French in David Batchelor, 'Art & Language. Ce que peindre veut dire' in the same issue of *Art Press*, p. 20. (This passage being omitted from the English original due to errors in laying out.)

people who continue to lay claim to it. According to Adorno, 'absolute freedom in art, always limited to the particular, comes into contradiction with the perennial unfreedom of the whole.'[19] But this offers only a partial explanation of the abandonment of aesthetic sovereignty that Catherine Francblin describes as follows: Ryman is 'led to celebrate—in chorus with such as Picabia, Villeglé, Tinguely, Art & Language, Buren, Philippe Thomas or Sherry Levine, the fall of the sovereign artist. In his passion for the real, he is compelled to make common cause with all those who, throughout the century, "argue for the necessary and paradoxical effacement of the artist".'[20] A 'passion for the real' cannot overcome a crucial obstacle: in art, the real is inaccessible; as Nelson Goodman has shown, what is presented to aesthetic perception is never more than 'a sample of reality' and hence a simulacrum that functions as a symbol. What is more, the effacement of the artist does not in any way restrict his/her freedom to choose the form, material, dimensions, colour, etc., of the work; it concerns only the techniques of dissimulation by which, precisely, one masks the arbitrariness of an art radically emancipated from any traditional canon.

Towards the middle of the nineteenth century, with the generation of Baudelaire, Flaubert and Manet, art rejected any extrinsic social function, adornment of power or conformity to established taste. Its logic then gradually came to be defined as the symbolization of singular experience. Among the inventors of autonomy, the triviality of the object—the provincial petite-bourgeoise raised to the status of Romantic heroine, the ugli-

---

19 Theodor W. Adorno, *Aesthetic Theory*, trans. Robert Hullot-Kentor (Minneapolis: University of Minnesota Press, 1997), p. 1.

20 Catherine Francblin, 'La passion du réel', *Art Press*, special issue, *L'histoire continue* (1992), p. 39, citing at the end the words of Jean-Marc Poinsot.

ness and vice of the city transfigured in the poem, the prostitute in the attitude of a queen of beauty—has both polemical and prideful implications: polemical with regard to social reality and prideful with regard to a newly discovered power that allows creation *ex nihilo* or almost. There is no longer any reality that cannot be transformed into a symbol. It is still this polemical attitude and this pride that animate not only the Cubist collages that transfigure trivial objects but also the readymade. What disappears in Duchamp is the concern that survived among the first generation of autonomous artists to win the splendour of the work from the inconsequentiality of its pretext. The triviality of the readymade nonetheless derives its power from its contrast with the work that is intended to astound. This contrast hardly existed after Duchamp and it was therefore necessary to discover other means of preserving the pluridimensionality and essential tension of the artwork.

Once art had broken with any extrinsic function, its logic came to be defined on the basis of the relationship between the artist's intention to 'make art'—what s/he does in fact produce—and the interpretations offered of it. Such autonomy was gained through a number of stages:

> 1. In the first phase, artists aspire to free themselves from religious and political tutelage; at issue is the constitution of a properly aesthetic *sphere*, beholden to its own logic. At this first level, art is autonomous only from the *social* and not from the aesthetic point of view, where the heritage of tradition remains powerful, in Baudelaire's poems as in Manet's paintings.
>
> 2. In the second phase, autonomy extends to *artistic language*. 'L'art pour l'art' and Symbolism seek to free their means of expression from external utility. From

Baudelaire to Mallarmé, from Manet to Cubism to Abstraction, art abandons referential language to develop a medium that is no longer immediately accessible to the public which must learn an artistic language ever renewed, at first idiosyncratic and difficult to understand, but which later comes to enrich the language of all.

3. In the third phase, thanks to the constitution of a separate language, art becomes sovereign: it appropriates non-aesthetic reality to aesthetic ends and, in a distancing, suggestive or irritant fashion, acts on everyday awareness; at this level, its sovereign autonomy is that of an artistic appropriation and intervention, the appropriation for artistic purposes of any elements of the real whatsoever, and provocative intervention in a social space whose expectations of art are disappointed and offended by each new radicalization of language.

(a) This sovereignty finds expression, first of all, vis-à-vis the traditional media of painting; from Cubism on, with its pasted paper and its object-paintings, its incorporation into the pictorial surface of objects of every kind, reflection turns on the process of *inclusion*. The derealization of trivial objects is paralleled by an aestheticization of the world; *any* object whatsoever can now be considered from an aesthetic point of view and be deployed as a symbol in unexpected contexts.

(b) Attention then turns to the mechanism of aesthetic recognition and the context of reception and exhibition. With Duchamp's urinal, the artist wins his autonomy with regard to the context of reception. He plays on the ease with which collectors and dealers accept the wave of the magic wand that the artist uses to transform the trivial object into an art object, which thereby acquires considerable commercial value. From this moment on, no longer in thrall to the functioning of the institutions, he maintains his autonomy through the sovereignty of his attribution or refusal of aesthetic value to one object or another. Thanks to such a reflexive relationship to the work of art, the artist is in a position to intervene critically in those contexts of reception and exhibition that he does not control. Depending on the targets chosen and the mode of intervention, art can thus be equally well put into the service of Dadaist provocation as of political denunciation. Conversely, the political content can become an aesthetic phenomenon, being neutralized as such and thus made acceptable to the art market. In his concern for rupture and subversion, the artist is naturally attracted by radical political positions; but by an irresistible logic, so long as he is not supported by a context of political mobilization, he ends up being tolerated as an unthreatening dissident and must endlessly seek new forms in order to escape such tolerance.

(c) In the contemporary context, finally, the autonomy of art expresses itself in two forms. Given that

> its subversive effect is essentially channelled by
> competent institutions, the artist can either ignore
> the context of reception and content himself with a
> sovereign communication of his experience, or
> exploit his power of critical suggestion or destabi-
> lization of ordinary perception. Whatever the
> choice, he may no longer expect to act directly on
> the political consciousness of the public, but only
> present thought-provoking images.

Sovereignty then takes the form of the deployment of the (autonomous) language of art in a heteronomous context. In dramatizing this situation, Peter Bürger speaks of the aporetic situation[21] of the contemporary artist, caught between the impossibility of returning to the autonomy that the artwork enjoyed before the politicization of art, and the impossibility of relaunching the avant-garde project that was generally considered to have failed. The project can however only be considered to have failed if one believes that all avant-garde art was motivated by a single desire to change the world through art.

The euphoria of avant-garde movements derived from a double conviction: that of being able to absorb everything into art, to aestheticize everything, and that of being able to transform the world in the name of the utopian demands of art, becoming a political force. What has been revealed as illusory is this infinite horizon of aesthetic 'coherence', incorporating any possible reality into its universe or tending to destabilize any non-aesthetic reality in the name of its own sovereignty. For reality on the whole has remained indifferent to these enterprises.

---

21 Peter Bürger, 'L'autonomie de l'art dans l'histoire', trans. P. Mésonnier, in exhibition cat-alogue *Where?* (Musée d'art moderne de Saint-Étienne, 1992), p. 21.

What is more, in all avant-garde art an interest in its forms of expression is always interposed between the work and any political impact—which is difficult to calculate. Far from being caught in an insoluble aporia, the contemporary artist knows that his autonomy has its being in a heteronomous context on which he can act only indirectly, either in elaborating his own vision through the materials proper to it, or by catching the eye and the mind and provoking reflection on a referential reality without ever knowing the result of this reflection. In order to put into question the automatisms of language and of everyday perception, he therefore enjoys sovereign command over his own proper logic while provoking a context of reception that falls outside his control.

For the public too is 'sovereign' in its own way. What does it expect of a work of art? 'Nothing,' say the twentieth-century partisans of 'make it new'; 'everything,' say their adversaries, defenders of the autonomy of taste. When Duchamp signed and presented his first urinal, he set in motion a logic of creative sovereignty whose origins and limits we are today beginning to apprehend. A profane urinal occupies the place of an object once sacred. In his signature, he refers to the property rights that make the work a commodity. Prefabricated, it denounces the myth of artistic craft, displacing the creative act to the level of the artist's gesture and idea, effecting the sovereign annexation to the domain of art of a derealized object.

Duchamp's gesture is addressed both to the institution that receives, manages, judges or excludes works, and to a public that believes it has immediate access to art without an institutional filter. He inaugurates a relationship of challenge between the artist and the institution, a challenge soon *integrated* by the latter yet still forgetful of the autonomy of the public. It forgets that any work is, first of all, only a claim for aesthetic recognition. The work makes a claim on our time and our attention; if it is not successful, it bores us, it wastes our time, it is a disappointment. Modern art, and then the avant-gardes, occulted this aspect, issuing the public—a priori, one might say—a certificate of incompetence. It is true that for more than a century now the general public has distinguished itself by its conservative rejection of all intervention, by its litany of 'That isn't art.' All of a sudden, artists became accustomed, wrongfully, to declaring of their own sovereign motion that 'This is art', no longer taking any account of the processes of recognition, or confidently saying to themselves that recognition would finally come. Since the end of the Second World War, this relationship between contemporary art and the artist has changed profoundly. Through the museums and their educational endeavours, a relatively broad public has acquired a taste for the ruptures and provocations of modern art.

Unlike their predecessors, the neo-avant-gardes were almost immediately welcomed by the institutions and accorded particular attention by private and public collections. At the same time, the ruptures do not have the same status; they are integrated into contemporary culture, and the public, rather than being shocked by the collusion between authorities and artists, may rather wish to understand the justification for the choices made. The artist, it is true, obeys only those rules that he imposes on himself; it should nevertheless be possible to reconstruct them and to assess their relevance, interest, scope and fecundity—criteria that call upon the exercise of 'aesthetic rationality'. Conversely, the public, to be capable of judging, has to start from a position of sympathy without which there will be no chance of discovering the integrity of a heterodox experience.

Art is not spared the differentiation undergone by the logic of modern culture. Its own conquest of autonomy is inscribed in the wider context of the specialization of social activities on the basis of their own logics. With the disappearance of religious tutelage and dependence on feudal powers, art, like science, law and morality, seeks to follow only its own rules. It is no accident that aesthetics, as a philosophical discipline in its own right, makes its appearance around the middle of the eighteenth century, simultaneous with the constitution of the public sphere of bourgeois society. It is around this time too that one sees a change in the style of art criticism and literary criticism: works are no longer judged on the basis of their conformity to the rules and their agreement with pre-established taste, but increasingly in the name of criteria that they themselves inaugurate. Hence, from Romanticism on, the claim to autonomy is doubled by a pretension to sovereignty; in other words, it is the artist—or at most the community of artists and expert critics—who decides what falls within the realm of art. It is only in recent years that this principle has been seriously put into question.

Pierre Bourdieu presents the genesis of aesthetic autonomy through an account of the post-Romantic generation of French writers and artists. In a chapter in *The Rules of Art* entitled 'The Conquest of Autonomy', he shows how Flaubert and Baudelaire made a powerful contribution to 'the constitution of the literary field as a world apart, subject to its own laws'.[22] In painting, he says, 'Manet will achieve a similar revolution.'[23] In the beginning, the claim to autonomy has an ethical connotation, which it will indeed never entirely lose: it is *'moral indignation* against all forms of submission to the forces of power or to the market',[24] in the name not of an absence of rules but of rules one has defined for oneself. It was a matter

---

22 Pierre Bourdieu, *The Rules of Art,* trans. Susan Emanuel (Cambridge: Polity Press, 1996), p. 48.

23 Ibid., p. 105.

24 Ibid., p. 60.

first of all of inventing 'that unprecedented social personage who is the modern writer or artist, a full-time professional, dedicated to one's work in a total and exclusive manner, indifferent to the exigencies of politics and to the injunctions of morality, and not recognizing any jurisdiction other than the norms specific to one's own art'.[25]

This break with public expectations provokes, first of all, a lag in recognition: 'as the autonomy of cultural production grows, the interval of time necessary for works to impress on the public (most of the time against the critics) the concomitant norms of their perceptions is seen to grow likewise.' One thus witnesses, Bourdieu continues, a 'temporal gap between supply and demand'.[26] This lag will characterize all innovative art, from the mid-nineteenth to the mid-twentieth century, and is accompanied by an ever-more radical rupture with the expectations of the public. Hence the obligation to endlessly invent new forms, the symbols each time of an autonomy regained. But at a second stage, which Bourdieu does not consider in *The Rules of Art,* the interval between each successive avant-garde's affirmation of autonomy through the rejection of the residual compromises of its predecessors becomes shorter and shorter.

For Bourdieu, the ambition that was at first concerned only with the authenticity of art engenders in fact a 'dialectic of distinction',[27] by virtue of which artists compete with each other by distinguishing themselves from their contemporaries as well as from their predecessors; this competition is exacerbated by an economic dynamic that develops in the market for cultural goods. Bourdieu does not draw a clear distinction between these two aspects, the *normative* (properly aesthetic) aspect of modern

---

25 Ibid., pp. 76–7.

26 Ibid., p. 82.

27 Ibid., p. 126.

artists' aspirations—their desire to follow only those rules that they have imposed on themselves—and the *empirical* aspect of competition, of distinction and rupture as functions of necessities extraneous to art that have less to do with artistic aspirations and more with a constraint imposed by the market, and as such undermining autonomy. The title *The Rules of Art* confounds in a single phrase the autonomous rules that artists impose on themselves and the rules they must follow to survive in the market; it is in this sense that Bourdieu writes that it is necessary to 'contest art *according to the rules of art*',[28] in other words, to respect certain rules of social acceptability in order to be recognized as an artist.

The only intrinsic relation between these two aspects is the fact that the market destroys the old relations of dependence in 'emancipating' artists from feudal patronage, replacing it with both the possibility of autonomy and a new dependence, this time on supply and demand. When Bourdieu speaks of 'symbolic capital' or of the 'symbolic power acquired in the observance of the rules of the functioning of the field',[29] he again confuses the normative authority of the artist or intellectual, acquired by the production of significant and accomplished work, with empirical authority, the result of a strategic position in the 'field', which does not necessarily relate to any particular degree of artistic competence. Similarly, the 'power of consecration'[30] can derive either from the authority proper to an expert or from a strategic position as critic, editor, gallery director, etc.

It is a fact that the heteronomy of market and patronage perpetually threatens to annul the gains of aesthetic autonomy. The danger increases as the ruptural dynamic is incorporated into the cultural policy of both

---

28 Ibid., p. 170.

29 Ibid., p. 221.

30 Ibid., p. 224.

markets and public institutions, as innovation becomes acceptable and generally expected. Rupture is then no longer the prerogative of the artist but is in a way managed by patrons, who may expect it or even require it in order to gain advantage in the art market or the political prestige associated with boldness and open-mindedness. At the beginnings of artistic autonomy, in the time of Flaubert and Manet, wealth of ones own was needed to survive the lack of demand for avant-garde works. In the twentieth century, at least during the long period that followed the Second World War, avant-garde work tended to benefit both from an economic advantage on the art market and from public renown. As a result, the fact of effecting a new rupture—e.g. by relegitimizing kitsch, pornography and the advertising denounced by the avant-garde purists—no longer necessarily corresponds to an artistic necessity but may rather be a response to external demand or an anticipation of the logic of the market.

One thus sees a double short-circuit of aesthetic autonomy. On the one hand, artistic radicalization, the rupture with an accepted form of art, tends to lose its original purpose—to bring about vital, illuminating experience, of profound contemporary relevance—to become an end in itself. Less indeed among the most creative artists than among those who seek to make a name for themselves through spectacular boldness, but, with the mediation of art by the mass media, it is these last that capture the eye of the general public and of an art criticism bereft of all criteria. On the other, the management of contemporary art by public institutions short-circuits the ethics of rupture proclaimed by the autonomous artist—the revolt against the injustice of existing institutions—through administrative control of his anarchic liberty. It is this double short-circuit that explains the reaction, of both hatred and official approval, to such manifestations as 'Buren's columns' or the Louvre Pyramid. To the extent that the artist has entered a new relationship with institutions and with a public that is in principle more open to innovation than in the age of Manet and Baudelaire, he can no longer claim to be the only one capable of deciding what deserves the name of art; what is more, the dynamic of rupture as an end in itself has lost its legitimacy. No longer being the representative of a high-risk revolt that rejects all traditional criteria, art can no more evade aesthetic judgement.

sovereignty and internal autonomy

In looking for a form to embody a way of seeing and thinking, the contemporary artist no longer encounters only the works of earlier or contemporaneous artists. These have always imposed norms on any creative endeavour, norms sometimes inescapable in their critique of earlier modes of expression. Some approaches thus appear unacceptable or quite simply old-fashioned. Seeking to express what is unique and original in his own vision, the artist finds himself invited to follow, or at least to take note of, a collective logic of art that is heterogeneous with respect to his own project and which can sometimes impose an empty radicalization. To what extent can one speak here of 'heteronomy'? The history of modern art is a sequence of choices that have developed 'by rebound' while apparently presenting a logic of reduction to the essential. It seems today that this logic is becoming exhausted, that there is no longer any sense in pursuing reduction beyond certain extremes: the white canvas, the readymade, the empty space, the written instruction. Does this then put into question the whole Modern artistic succession and its logic?

'The slightest revision of judgment bearing on a key figure of modern art,' writes de Duve, 'runs the risk of carrying in its wake the auto-da-fé of the whole of Modernism . . . because no work of art exists alone, being always the interpretation of at least one other work. What makes Manet, Cézanne or Lissitzky key figures is also what binds them together.'[31] It remains to be seen whether this logic, the logic of a progression towards the essential, remains binding for contemporary art, or whether a one-way street to a point of no return has not been replaced by a multiplicity of reflections, critical stances and dialogues.

De Duve says again, 'Everything begins and ends in aesthetic judgment,'[32] but he believes this judgement is answerable to the actual history of art. He declares himself to be against

> the old ideology of the autonomy of art, according to which artworks can perfectly well dispense with theories and interpretations: that being sufficient unto themselves, they enjoy complete immunity and impunity with regard to what critics and art historians may have to say abut them. This is not true. Artworks have everything to do with theories and interpretations . . . they themselves are theoretical and interpretive.[33]

Yet the 'old ideology of the autonomy of art'—which does not imply an asocial reclusion but rather a proper logic of art's own, including when it steps out onto theoretical and political terrain—is making a comeback, fair and square. The work of art is distinguished from the aesthetic judgement by the irreducibility of its medium, of its mode of symbolization. Even the 'concept' of conceptual art is not purely discursive, as is witnessed by the spatial staging of the discourse.

---

31 Thierry de Duve, 'Who's Afraid of Red, Yellow and Blue: Barnett Newman Between Modernism and Post-Modernism', *ArtForum* 22/1 (September 1983), p. 34.

32 Ibid., p. 35.

33 Ibid.

By the same token, the public and the critics rediscover their own freedom of judgement. As in the political domain, artistic authority, which is losing the appearance of the 'sacred' that it retained in the myths of the avant-garde, has to be founded in motivated recognition. Even in avant-garde art, and *a fortiori* in contemporary art, works can be rich or poor, successes or failures, academic or original, profound or flat. If the tension between the sovereignty of art (the freedom to select elements of the world, obsessions, unprecedented perceptions, wrenched from reality and transformed into symbols in accordance with the artist's logic) and the point [*enjeu*] of the work (the presentation of significant experience) is abandoned, there remains only an empty aspiration to bring about another turn of the screw in the spiral of radicalization. 'Sovereignty' threatens to empty autonomy of its meaning. It is a question of maintaining the freedom to give expression to acute, vital and still unacceptable experiences; today, formal innovation is often the driver of a heteronomous escalation without experiential content.

In this situation, the public's relationship to art changes once again. At first, autonomous art sought to break with the public, to no longer meet its expectations, so as to be free to present what seemed essential. Later, the cultivated public accepted this logic of rupture and made an effort to follow its discontinuous progress; like artists themselves, they acquired a taste for ever-new provocations. Surrealism, Abstraction, Abstract Expressionism, Pop Art—all gained a public in little time. But later still, the public refused to go along with a radicalization now *required.*

When rupture is planned, presenting only an idea that could equally be expressed in a few words, without need of the density of the artistic symbol, when the conflictual relation between art and the public is short-circuited by an interested complicity between patrons and artists, when works whose scale would prevent them ever being installed in a private collection are directly created for the museum, and when finally these monumental works have no other goal than to deliberately fail to meet expectations, we have witnessed a revolt by critics who endeavour to represent the cultivated general public. The public remembers that it too is autonomous, that it has 'rights' vis-à-vis the work of art, and that it can turn its back on the latter if it no longer speaks to it. Firstly, the public is free to show an interest in a work of art or not. Secondly, it can require of it, as soon as it demands their attention, that it meets a number of requirements. Certain postmodern tendencies, Neo-Expressionist or cultivating kitsch in the second degree, exploit this breach opened by an empty radicalization. They present the other, regressive face of the double risk perpetually run by modern art: empty radicalization, or an attempt to escape the demands inherited from the Modernist movements.

Since Duchamp, as we have seen, the idea has got around that the artist has the sovereign freedom to define as art what he presents, simply because he, the artist, designates it as such; hence the idea, pregnant with consequences, of the readymade, 'that manufactured object promoted to the dignity of an art object by the artist's symbolic stroke'.[34] 'Knowing the game to his fingertips,' Bourdieu writes of Duchamp, 'he produces objects whose production as works of art presupposes the production of the producer as artist.'[35] In other words, it is thanks to his authority as an artist, acquired otherwise than by the readymade, that Duchamp is able to exercise his aesthetic authority outside the domains of the painter's or sculptor's craft, conferring upon it his gaze, his idea, his power to name and to attribute the status of art to the things that he takes from the real.

---

34 Bourdieu, *The Rules of Art*, pp. 246–7.

35 Ibid., p. 246.

Repeated with variations and without substantial innovation, this idea too falls victim to the constant rupture with past radicalism. With Minimal and Conceptual Art, with the neutral object and the idea without material density, the spiral of radicalization arrives at its nadir. The art of rupture can then renew itself, without turning back, only by going beyond empty sovereignty: towards the human body, irreducible to a work of art, to its spatial and social environment, to cosmic nature that escapes the artist's control. But this is no longer the presentation of a coherence constructed by the artist, but an allusion to a meaning external to art. This impasse results from the fact that both sovereignty and the dynamic of rupture tend to lose their original purpose, establishing themselves as ends in themselves and replacing vital experience with an idea about the history of art.

The meaning of the readymade is disputed.[36] It was not intended or designed as an artwork, and it is only afterwards that its integration into the museum consecrated it as such, neutralizing its attack on the 'institution of art'. Its non-art aspect, the intention to highlight the mysteries of the everyday, the trivial, the incongruous, to draw attention to life itself, has to be respected. But the readymade also shows that it is not so easy to escape from 'art' so long as one remains within the context of the art exhibition, of the object isolated from its context and offered to contemplation, in other words, so long as an object is presented in the place traditionally occupied by the work of art.

De Duve, who thinks of it as 'art about art',[37] reproaches Greenberg for 'not seeing that Duchamp, in inventing the readymade, did not at all

---

36 Thierry de Duve, *Au nom de l'art, Pour une archéologie de la modernité* (Paris: Éditions de Minuit, 1989), and the same author's *Résonances du readymade*.

37 de Duve, *Résonances du readymade*, p. 15.

seek to extend aesthetic judgement and artistic appropriation as far as possible beyond the conventions of painting but was rather registering the fact that the invention of photography had radically altered all the conditions of artistic enunciation within the pictorial conventions.'[38] De Duve is right to dispute the idea of a 'sovereignty of art' understood as 'an extension of artistic appropriation and aesthetic judgment'. In fact, the 'sovereignty of art' does not mean that at any given moment anything can become art; that would suggest an empty arbitrariness. It is rather a matter of a double movement—of extension and withdrawal. Once aesthetic 'sovereignty' sees itself obliged to abandon an art practice and become academic, a return is not possible without further justification. So this is not an extension in the sense of an increase in concrete possibilities. The freedom of contemporary art is constantly burning its boats, but the burning of boats is not in itself sufficient to establish a bridgehead in the history of art.

---

[38] de Duve, 'Ryman irreproductible', *Essais datés 1*.

criticism's dereliction of duty:
criticism, aesthetics and the history of art

Faced with the difficulties of giving an account of contemporary art, there are two easy ways out: either to adopt the objectivizing approach of the historian who simply records the choices of galleries, museums and well-known critics or to register ones own subjective preferences—rarely at odds with prevailing estimations—without attempting to justify them, two stances that are only too easily combined when the preferences are those implicitly expressed by those who have the institutional power to acquire and to exhibit or to speak and to write about artworks. Criticism then finds itself neutralized, its place taken by authoritative declarations, interviews and collusive presentations.

Criticism, whose task is to justify admiration or disapproval of a work by informed argument and interpretation, has to be distinguished from aesthetics and the history of art. Art criticism and art history are indeed complementary, but antagonistic in their principles. Though critical judgement may not aspire to historical 'objectivity' or modestly content itself with the collection of significant facts, it will nonetheless be a poor thing if it is not historically informed, 'pressurized', as Greenberg puts it, by familiarity with art.[39] And while the history of art can itself become criticism when it re-evaluates older work in the light of the implicit history of its innovative successors, it is more commonly a convenient way of avoiding it.

Aesthetics often claims the right to stand in judgement on criticism, while criticism for its part can easily wonder what the point is of aesthetics or the philosophy of art.[40] A spontaneous relationship to the work, pleasure and displeasure, feeling or technical interest, the discovery of meaning or the sharing of experience, interpretation or judgement—none of these seems to require resort to aesthetics;[41] there thus exists a solid anti-philosophical tradition among critics and art-lovers. Aesthetics can seem a pedantic exercise that involves empty reconstruction without reference to any particular work, of our relationship to art, to the beautiful, to the sublime.

If aesthetics suspends the immediate relationship to the artwork, it does this for at least two reasons. It may endeavour, on the one hand, to identify a logic of its own, distinct from the cognitive and the moral, making it possible to set aside works or judgements governed by a logic other than aesthetic, or at least to isolate the logic of an approach that takes certain objects as aesthetic rather than useful or otherwise, informative, valuable, etc. Or it may, on the other hand, be concerned about interrogating the limits of the beautiful and of art and about reflecting on the significance of this type of phenomenon for individual and social life.

---

39 de Duve, *Essais datés 1*, p. 110.

40 Paul Ardenne, review of *L'Art sans compas* in *Art Press* 178 (March 1993), p. 73: 'a field decidedly incapable of autonomy, constrained to set its compass by art itself—an art that for its own part can easily do without aesthetics.'

41 See, for example, Michel Makarius, 'Au plaisir des oeuvres' in Roger-Paul Droit, *L'art est-il une connaissance?* (Paris: Le Monde éditions, 1993), pp. 29–36.

Criticism draws freely on the conceptual definitions of different systems of aesthetics, without being rigorously tied to any, taking philosophical metatheory as the doctrine of a historically situated movement. Aesthetics as such becomes 'Romantic, Symbolist, avant-gardist, Minimalist or post-modern aesthetics'.[42] It is a legitimate blindness in criticism to remain unaware of the theoretical status of aesthetic concepts, reducing them to labels restricted to certain historical trends. Conversely, it is a blindness proper to philosophical aesthetics to claim to formulate general concepts independent of the historical transformations of the concept of art, excluding certain forms of art simply because they fall outside its categories. As is shown, for example, by Clement Greenberg's negative reaction to Minimal Art, such limitation characterizes criticism too when it accepts the definition of art that underlies a single type of historic art.

Kant tried to formulate the logic of our relationship to the beautiful and to art. For the Romantic aestheticians who succeeded him, art had a more important position in philosophic thought. They were convinced that 'art must replace a defective philosophical discourse.'[43] Art was sacralized, and even became the last line of defence of a residual 'sacred'. For Kant had opened a breach that would be exploited by the Jena Romantics. Art, and poetry in particular, was for him a 'quasi-sacred' that the Romantics had only to strip of the reservation. But the metaphysical regression in this speculative turn should not blind one to the advance it represents in understanding the specificity of art. In considering only the Romantics' ontology, one neglects their discoveries regarding the structure

---

42 'There is an Impressionist taste and a Cubist taste. But the *fact* of taste is invariable. The true art-lover adapts to tastes as contradictory as Rubens and Ingres, Memling and Pollock' (de Duve, *Essais datés 1*, p. 108).

43 Jean-Marie Schaeffer, *Art of the Modern Age: Philosophy of Art from Kant to Heidegger*, trans. S. Randall (Princeton, NJ: Princeton University Press, 2000), p. 69.

of the work of art. These concern, on the one hand, its reflexive character which, unlike natural beauty, is itself reflected, constructed upon a claim to achievement, to recognition of its status as an artwork by a criticism capable of according it; and on the other, the nature of the 'speech' [*parole*] of the artwork, not simply as an utterance but in the sense of its irreducibility to the universal rules of a language. Every work is constituted on the basis of rules that are valid only for itself, for a single case.

What escapes a positivist or empiricist view of aesthetic judgement as an expression of pleasure is, first of all, the idea of the shared, inherent in the very pragmatics of the term 'beauty' or, indeed, in the logic of aesthetics. When we experience an aesthetic pleasure, we go beyond the domain of private sensation that is merely sensual pleasure. For this pleasure implies the recognition of a justifiable claim; when one finds a work of art beautiful or successful it is always for reasons. What can be saved of the Kantian aesthetics, it seems, is the notion of a normative bond between persons who can see the reasons why a work claims to be aesthetically successful; it includes an intersubjective necessity designated by the qualifier 'beautiful' or 'successful' when knowingly employed as an aesthetic judgement.

The Romantics, on the other hand, inaugurate a mode of knowledge both regressive and novel: regressive in returning to a metaphysics criticized by Kant, and novel in its grasp of phenomena that escape nomological or empirical understanding which call for methods appropriate to the understanding of individuals and their signifying production: works of art and historical phenomena. At first, this type of understanding—in linguistic terms, of speech, not of language—took the form of a return to metaphysics. But the aesthetic logic thus discovered is not necessarily bound to such a return and, through a long and difficult apprenticeship, modern thought has begun to rid itself of these regressive elements. It was also necessary that the confusion of aesthetics and criticism brought about by the Romantics be resolved through the drawing of a distinction between aesthetic logic itself and its practical deployment in confrontation with a work of art.

After the Romantics, Benjamin contributed to this process, though not bringing it to a final conclusion, by illuminating a number of interesting dead-ends. In his book on German Romanticism, he describes the way in which the Romantic theorists developed certain principles of modern criticism. Schlegel and Novalis start from the Kantian and Fichtean idea of self-consciousness, then transpose reflection into the domain of art. Just like the subject, for them the work of art cannot be objectified in the manner of an object of science—of physics, more particularly—but has to be seen as an interlocutor in an intersubjective relationship. The work of art is not just an object of reflection, it is itself a site of possessing and critique and so a kind of subject or at least a configuration having an intentional structure. It reflects on and criticizes itself; it is conceived not simply as a function of crude sensation or raw emotion—which would be the sign of dilettantism, not of art—but according to certain rational criteria whose import may be reconstructed. Consequently, aesthetic judgement in the name of 'taste' is transformed into 'the judgment of works by immanent criteria'.[44] This shift from taste to immanent critique has a double implication. On the one hand, it involves the emancipation of criticism from the prejudices of 'good taste' or of a historically determined 'horizon of expectation', while on the other it confers on it a metaphysical status. As Benjamin goes on to say, 'criticism in its central intention is not judgment but, on the one hand, the completion, consummation and system-

---

44 Walter Benjamin, 'The Concept of Criticism in German Romanticism', in Marcus Bullock and Michael W. Jennings (eds), *Selected Writings, 1913–1926*, VOL. 1, trans. David Lachterman, Howard Eiland and Ian Balfour (Cambridge, MA: Harvard University Press, 1996), p. 155.

atization of the work and, on the other hand, its resolution in the absolute,'[45] in other words, in the Idea of art.

One understands, then, why, after Romanticism, aesthetics could be reduced to criticism: from the moment aesthetic judgement gave way to the interpretation of the work understood as the supreme source of truth, aesthetics was no longer any more than the elementary method of a criticism that discovered the philosophic truth by interrogating the work of art. Hence the career of a philosophically ambitious criticism, with Benjamin and Adorno, Heidegger and Bataille, Sartre and Barthes, Deleuze and Derrida. In France, this tradition finds itself superimposed on another—the tradition that from Diderot and Baudelaire has privileged criticism anchored in the work over the generalities of the philosophy of art, considered to be empty and abstract. Imperceptibly, French criticism has thus moved on from the subtle essay of the connoisseur and the aesthete to a speculative overload, an ambitious commentary on works of art that virtually replaces philosophy. It was perhaps to escape this overload that the later Roland Barthes broke with an aesthetics of binding judgement to speak in the first person.

According to the Romantics, the work should in principle be judged henceforth only according to immanent criteria; thus, there can be no negative criticism, only criticizable and uncriticizable works. This is the reason Benjamin will modify the Romantic theory by introducing the concept of 'truth-content', which brings with it the possibility of negative judgement. But 'truth' here relates to a philosophico-theological doctrine, which, unlike the Romantic conception, no longer depends on art itself; for Benjamin, on the contrary, such a doctrine can in our age be glimpsed only through the power of 'naming' inherent in works of art, a feature of

---

45 Ibid., p. 159.

human language lost in the inflationary expansion of 'signification'. Such a sacralizing conception of criticism may still be encountered today in authors who draw their inspiration from Heidegger, or Benjamin, or both.

The essay on 'The Work of Art in the Age of Mechanical Reproduction' is the starting point for another reading of the relationship between aesthetics and criticism. In this essay, Benjamin pushes as far as it will go the notion of a radical desacralization of art, making of the artwork something entirely new, a means of adapting to technological civilization and facing up to the social conflicts that it engenders. Here it is no longer a question of judging works of art in the name of immanent criteria, but in the name of a political project to place art at the service of social transformation. What is in question here is no longer the aesthetic quality of artworks—an occasion for a meditative contemplation inherited from religious practice—but their social and political utility. From such an instrumental point of view, works of art are either a means of perceptual education or symptoms to be translated into political knowledge; they are not works appreciated for their aesthetic qualities. Hence the invitation to 'wake' from this dream that is contemporary civilization as constructed since the mid-nineteenth century. For the sake of this awakening, the destruction of all aesthetic criteria—traditional or otherwise—seems not only legitimate but necessary and desirable, while the theological celebration of the authentic work still depended on such criteria.

In the spirit of the avant-garde, and of Brecht especially, Benjamin reduces the aesthetic interest of a work to its conformity with an ever-higher level of technology. In this sense, Dada is overtaken by the very technique of film: 'Dadaism endeavoured to create by pictorial—and literary—means the effects which the public today seeks in the film.'[46] Taken

---

[46] Walter Benjamin, 'The Work of Art in the Age of Mechanical Reproduction', in *Illuminations*, trans. Harry Zorn (London: Pimlico, 1999), p. 230.

45

literally, Benjamin's essay condemns in advance the artistic explorations of the post-War period—Abstract Expressionism, Pop Art, Minimal Art, Conceptual Art—as outdated compared to cinematographic technique, for their still being beholden to the aesthetic 'aura', to the uniqueness that makes them cultic objects.[47] Only the technique of reproduction, he says, can reach the masses who have the right of access to art.

The desacralization of art is thus accompanied here by a de-aestheticization that does away with any specifically aesthetic logic. To the extent that aesthetic criteria of quality are replaced, through knowledge and perceptual adaptation, by criteria of socio-political efficacity, a Chaplin film, by virtue of its higher technical level, is necessarily superior to a painting by Picasso: 'Mechanical reproduction of art changes the reaction of the masses toward art. The reactionary attitude toward a Picasso painting changes into the progressive reaction toward a Chaplin movie.'[48]

This point of view is defensible only to the extent that the desacralization of art is paralleled not only by a politicization of art but also by a politicization of the 'masses' themselves. In such a case, a new solidarity would come to replace that which disappeared alongside the tradition on which the aura was based. We would arrive at a post-capitalist society based on the new solidarity of the 'masses' in the 'communism'[49] invoked by the first version of the essay. Art could assume a merely political function, in so far as its aesthetic functions, not lending themselves to public use, would have lost all interest and legitimacy.

Much avant-garde art has indeed been created on this basis. Notably in the context of the neo-avant-gardes, conformity with the logic of rupture

---

47 Ibid., p. 217.

48 Ibid., p. 227.

49 Walter Benjamin, *Gesammelte Schriften*, VOL. 1/2 (Frankfurt am Main: Suhrkampf, 1974), p. 469.

with the traditional functions of art has replaced the demands that one would earlier have made on a work. De Duve was able to say of Yves Klein and his sale of 'zones of immaterial pictorial sensibility'—voids certified as artistic—that 'he did a considerable wrong to the avant-gardes (a retroactive wrong, one name of which is neo-avant-garde).'[50] To play with the power of aesthetic inauguration threatens to discredit contemporary art as a whole.

This short-circuit between politics and aesthetics, which eliminates the categories of aesthetic evaluation, cuts the last links between criticism and aesthetics. For artistic projects content to intervene in the mechanisms of artistic reception, properly aesthetic considerations no longer have any *raison d'être*. It is now not a matter of proposing an aesthetic experience but of unmasking, ironizing and increasing vigilance with regard to institutional contexts, often indeed with the complicity of the institutions themselves. Certain works of visual art which, unlike their literary or musical counterparts, are unique works having a market value, have a very specific status, but the meaning of a work of art cannot be reduced to any artist's particular attitude towards the commodity fetishism that attaches to them as objects.

This was realized by Benjamin who, later for the most part, abandoned the call for radical desacralization and the elimination of aesthetic criteria. It seems in fact that there is in Benjamin's work an important break, occurring some months after the completion of *The Work of Art* in 1935. Two of his texts in particular, *The Storyteller* (1936) and *On Some Motifs in Baudelaire* (1939), evidence a concern to salvage aesthetic criteria independent of political evaluation. In abandoning political hope in the 'masses', Benjamin gives up any justification of art based on technical reproduction, and he has to reintroduce aesthetic categories.

---

50 Thierry de Duve, 'Yves Klein or the Dead Dealer', *October* 49/3 (1989), pp. 72–90.

In one sense, then, Benjamin never approached art from a specifically aesthetic point of view. Whether in the name of philosophico-theological 'doctrine', political commitment, the dynamic of the forces of production, or finally a theory of historical experience, he always turns to extra-artistic issues in assessing the importance and value of works of art. To the question 'What do we rightly call beautiful?' he was able to reply only by referring to the ancestral experience of cult and ritual; this he abandoned in the name of politics, but only temporarily, before attempting to rescue the memory of an occulted tradition. But this beauty is not that of constructed works of art, whether successful or otherwise, but that of the vision of history that Benjamin considers to be the most authentic.

destabilization

The disappearance of any normative idea of art, of any conception of an art that 'has to be made', as a consequence of its 'sovereignty', has had its effect on art criticism; much more, in any case, than on literary criticism. Even if 'modern art isn't just anything. Full stop,'[51] it now has hardly any criteria to justify its judgements. Sometimes, it proudly boasts of this total freedom, the absence of any criterion, the latter synonymous with prohibition. Sometimes, it attempts to compensate for that absence through a conception of aesthetic 'jurisprudence'[52] or case-law embodied in the con-

---

51 de Duve, *Au nom de l'art*, p. 122.

52 Ibid., pp. 36ff., 50ff., 114; p. 51ff.: 'Jurisprudence is the historicity immanent in your practice as a historian. It passes on to you the documents recording the judgments of your predecessors and will pass on the record of yours to your successors. It does not as such offer the theoretical form of historicity. And the other name for jurisprudence, correcting notions of both style and avant-garde, is tradition.'

secration of a work by art history. But to take history as authority is to abandon the effort to rationally justify ones judgements and choices. And as for the alternative that involves the substitution of criteria of political lucidity for those of aesthetics,[53] it is incapable of identifying the artistic specificity of the political positions it considers to be correctly taken.

Critics thus generally content themselves with indicating their preferences, describing what they see, as if the interest of the work would then be evident, or rehearsing the statements of artists themselves, as if it were for them to define the meaning and importance of their works, as if, indeed, since the age of Conceptual Art, or even since Duchamp, the gap between the creation and analysis of art had virtually disappeared.[54] Since the readymade and the 'concept' have given the impression that art was within everyone's reach, only the cult of the artist, of the artist's statement, his personal theory, his attitude, his staging of himself, seems to be able to maintain the distance between art and trivial reality, between the artwork with its critical and evocative power and its inert double.

If it stands in solidarity with contemporary art, criticism tends to avoid the notions of the failed or mediocre work. When it does not take up a position of passionate hostility in the name of a traditional concep-

---

53 Benjamin Buchloh, in the introduction to his *Essais historiques II*, trans. C. Gintz (Villeurbanne: Art Édition, 1992), p. 9.

54 'When criticism claims to be art, it is no longer prepared to submit itself to intellectual judgment, and all sorts of falsifications of the facts "as they came about", all sorts of betrayals become possible. There have also been examples of a symmetrical danger when art takes the form of criticism. It may happen that an artist seeks to reduce all art, not only his own, but that of others as well, to a critical discourse, regurgitating this discourse as a work of art. The case of conceptual art, mainly that of Joseph Kosuth and *Art & Language*, is a prime example of this attitude and is probably largely responsible for the traumatisms the avant-garde is undergoing today and their various regressive consequences' (de Duve, 'Who's Afraid of Red, Yellow and Blue?' p. 35).

tion of art, it becomes the artist's spokesperson, interviewer and impresario. When it does not content itself with repeating artists' accounts of themselves, it often merely comments on them, illustrating a preconceived philosophy through the works. According to Judd,

> An article is usually written by a fan of the artist . . . Rarely is an artist's work seriously evaluated: great, good, middling, bad, awful, nothing. An artist never has certain virtues and some limitations. No-one says an artist is a secondary artist, which isn't a bad achievement in the long run.[55]

For want of criteria of evaluation, criticism—when it isn't philosophical commentary, which also allows one to avoid any judgement of value[56]—becomes positivist, contenting itself with the minute description of works, without any attempt to interpret, situate or critique,[57] which might entail making negative assessments, hurting artists and their reputations and worrying their galleries, collectors and public patrons. Reflection on artistic success and aesthetic significance is displaced by a general expert interest in everything a rated artist does, taken in a way as the abundant symptoms of creativity, as if it were impossible to identify a project behind them and more or less successful endeavours to bring it to reality. At the same time,

---

55 Donald Judd, 'A long discussion not about master-pieces but about why there are so few of them: Part II', *Art in America* 72/9 (October 1984), p. 10.

56 See Jacques Derrida, 'Cartouches' in *The Truth in Painting*, trans. Geoff Bennington and Ian McLeod (Chicago: University of Chicago Press, 1987), pp. 183–247, and Georges Didi-Huberman, *Ce que nous voyons, ce qui nous regarde* (Paris: Éditions de Minuit, 1992).

57 While literary criticism has retained a strongly evaluative bent, art criticism in *Art Press* has become more and more 'positivist' in this sense since the eighties. While the shift to a less polemical or partisan stance is in many ways to be welcomed, it is in itself no replacement for a demanding critique.

the public displays a general lack of interest in an artistic production whose significance escapes it and which is thrown into doubt, as a whole, by the absence of hierarchy. The emancipation of contemporary art from all traditional criteria has opened up a field of limitless possibilities and total freedom, but has also helped to discredit it; the absence of normative requirements has a counterpart in the hostile indifference of the uninitiated.

This failure of criticism is not simply the result of institutional pressures; it derives too from art's post-Duchampian power of self-definition, echoed in theories such as those of Goodman, who defines art without reference to any notion of quality.[58] Yet as de Duve correctly reminds us:

> Quality, aesthetic pleasure, the judgment of taste—the three expressions are synonymous—are the main thing for an art critic. Or his job, which in the end is to expound what he likes, makes no sense. That the notion of aesthetic quality is suspect—and suspect more particularly of idealism—should not prevent him from making use of it without shame, because it is—under whatever name—what always makes the difference in the end.[59]

The entire problem is to know how it is that 'to expound what you like' could at the same time be to formulate an appropriate judgement of 'quality' that is not purely and simply an expression of subjective preference. And the difficulty is exacerbated by the rule of 'anything at all'. Retrospectively, it is always relatively easy to measure the impact of a work by its influence on successors and to derive from this an aesthetic judge-

---

58 Nelson Goodman, *Ways of Worldmaking* (Hassocks: Harvester, 1978), p. 66.

59 de Duve, 'Ryman irreproductible', *Essais datés 1*, p. 128.

ment. This is not the case when this 'judgement of history' has not been given or when revision proves necessary.

The unease is all the greater today, confronted with a logic of artistic development that leads either to the negation of art, or to what Danto calls an awareness of its structures, of its essence, in Warhol's *Brillo Boxes*, for example.[60] Like Benjamin in 1936, we have the sense that a spiral of radicalization has come to an end, and that the ejection of aesthetic categories was justified only by a political or philosophical project, a project today dated and cogently criticized. Above all, art is not the most appropriate way of revolutionizing society. Its field of intervention is too limited, its effects too uncertain and ambiguous; in endeavouring to deprive the public of any satisfaction, it no longer has any emancipatory effect. Of avant-garde subversion, Habermas could say in 1980 that 'ironically, the radical attempt to sublate art reinstates those categories with which classical aesthetics had circumscribed its own domain.'[61] For the attempt to translate art into life through the desublimation of forms or the politicization of content only deprives the works of all aesthetic content; 'once meaning has been desublimated and form dismantled nothing remains and no emancipatory effect results.'[62] There remains the question: how do we get out of this impasse confronting both criticism and aesthetics? Is it enough to return to the categories of traditional aesthetics, or have these,

---

60 Arthur C. Danto, *The Transfiguration of the Commonplace: A Philosophy of Art* (Cambridge, MA: Harvard University Press, 1981), p. vii: 'I should like to believe that with the Brillo boxes the possibilities are objectively closed and that the history of art has come, in a way, to an end.'

61 Jürgen Habermas, 'Modernity: An Unfinished Project' in Seyla Benhabib and Maurizio Passerin d'Entrèves (eds), *Habermas and the Unfinished Project of Modernity*, trans. Nicholas Walker (Cambridge, MA: MIT Press, 1997), p. 49.

62 Ibid.

as Habermas says, 'changed their character in the process',[63] or again, do they require further transformation and if so, in what way?

In France, one can identify three distinct varieties of contemporary aesthetics: one which endeavours to continue the avant-gardist project without any precise political ambition, turning it into a subversive non-conformism; an anti-avant-gardist reaction that attempts to rewrite the history of modern art since Impressionism, or even since Romanticism; and a positivist neutralization of modernity in the name of a value-free descriptivism inspired by analytic philosophy and structuralist poetics. These three complementary attitudes have no direct equivalents in other countries, while positions found elsewhere in the world are but feebly represented in France—the differentiated awareness of modernity or the frankly archaic and reactionary anti-modernism that one finds in France too in the fields of history and political theory.

Three types of reproach are thus addressed to contemporary art:

> 1. That it wishes to be accepted 'en bloc', allowing neither distinction nor hierarchy among artworks (J.-P. Domecq).[64] This period of art believes, in fact, that it has done away with the need for aesthetic criteria. It remains to be seen whether its art is to be judged according to traditional criteria of taste and satisfaction, or whether these criteria must be redefined if works of contemporary art are to be understood and evaluated.

> 2. That much modern and contemporary art, it is said, is based on a category mistake, more especially on a confu-

---

63 Ibid.

64 Jean-Phillippe Domecq speaks of a 'prohibition on categorization' and appeals for 'discernment', in 'L'Art contemporain contre l'art moderne', *Esprit* 185 (October 1992), p. 5.

sion of art and science that entails a misunderstanding of the specific vocation of art (O. Céna).[65] Calls are made for an art that offers 'meaning', an 'experience of the presence of the entirely present [*tout présent*]', and an encounter between the 'sensuous body' and the 'sensuous body of the world' (Le Bot).[66] It is hardly ever asked why so many of this century's artists have chosen to renounce this kind of sensuous experience and to disturb our perceptual expectations. Certain philosophers would add that this part of modern art, and the avant-gardes in particular, make a false claim to absolute truth, a claim inherited from Romantic philosophy, by virtue of which art appoints itself judge of the contemporary world (L. Ferry,[67] J. M. Schaeffer).[68] These criticisms are justified in

---

65 Olivier Céna, 'Le blanc souci de rien', *Télérama,* special issue, *Art contemporain: le grand bazar* (October 1992), pp. 11ff., 15ff.

66 Marc Le Bot, 'Pensée artistique et logique sérielle', *Esprit* 185 (October 1992), p. 29.

67 Luc Ferry, *Homo Aestheticus*: *The Invention of Taste in the Democratic Age*, trans. Robert de Loaiza (Chicago: University of Chicago Press, 1993), p. 191: 'the new [Nietzschean] classicism that makes of the truth unconcealed by the work of art a difference, no longer an identity, will find its vocation in the "avant-gardes" which . . . fascinate contemporary philosophy.' In the spirit of the neo-conservative thinker Daniel Bell (*The Cultural Contradictions of Capitalism,* New York: Basic Books, 1976), Ferry attacks avant-garde and contemporary art, denouncing the 'hedonism' and 'narcissism' of contemporary society, which, for him, are putting into question the humanist tradition (pp. 200ff.). As if conversion to a more 'humanist' art would bring about the disappearance of the dissonant experience that finds expression in the art of the period. See my article 'L'esthétique, l'individualisme et la tentation néoconservatrice', *Critique* 521 (October 1990), pp. 785–801.

68 Schaeffer, *Art of the Modern Age*, pp. 271ff. See also my article 'Esthétiques hédonistes', *Critique* 540 (May 1992), pp. 353–73.

so far as they target the excessive philosophical pretensions of artworks and art criticism, but on the other hand they tend to underestimate the cognitive dimension of modern art. In the same way, the uncomfortable aspects of contemporary art, upon which aesthetic dogmatism pinned its critical ambitions, are reduced to ideological prejudices and treated as more or less illegitimate.

3. Benefiting from both the absence of criteria and the confusion between art and science that allows artists in the name of the 'avant-garde' to cultivate innovation as such, these critics say, certain highly-regarded contemporary artists (Warhol, Beuys, Buren) are marked in particular by the pernicious or ill-understood influence of Marcel Duchamp, and are completely over-rated, over-priced or even worthless, owing their reputation to self-publicity or to a form of guilt-tripping blackmail of anti-avant-gardism (J.-P. Domecq).[69] The force of this criticism is diminished by hasty or even abusive generalization. Such denunciation of contemporary art as a hoax pure and simple is powerless, taking no account of the fact that a return to a more 'normal', traditional and expressive language that keeps to the confines of the easel-painting is not a matter of simple decision, otherwise artists would be producing such works in great numbers, as an expression of intergenerational dissent, and no institutional conspiracy could stop it.

---

69 Jean-Phillippe Domecq, 'La crise de l'art contemporain' in *Esprit,* February 1992, p. 36: 'frauds as big as Warhol, Buren, Schnabel, Stella, Rosenquist, Garouste, Supports-Surfaces'; 'work as worthless as Warhol's', etc.; see also the same author's *Artistes sans art?* (Paris: Éditions Esprit, 1994).

In opposition to modern, avant-garde or contemporary movements, a certain aesthetics, in a return to traditional philosophical 'basics', is re-establishing a metatheory of taste, pleasure and sensibility. Setting its time machine into motion, it locates in Nietzsche, or even in Kant or the Romantics, the source of the modern perversion: the moment when aesthetics compromised its specificity in laying claim to truth and aping science or metaphysics.

For some years now, a wind of reaction and general questioning has been blowing through the theory of art. After Jean Clair, once curator of a Duchamp exhibition at the Pompidou and today a convert to Bonnard and Balthus, certain journals such as *Esprit* have devoted special issues to the subject, hostile to contemporary art and more especially to the caricatural epigones of the avant-gardes. In one such, published on the occasion of the FIAC in 1992, one reads: 'And so Pop Art, Hyperrealism and Minimal Art appeared in the United States in opposition to Abstract Expressionism, and then Conceptual in opposition to Minimal Art, or in France to the New Realists . . . then BMTP . . . then Supports/Surface . . . At best, they are subversive, like Pop Art and the New Realists, but so fascinated by what they denounce (consumer society) that their impact is no more than that of a little society scandal, like Andy Warhol, who for want of anything better holds up his own cynicism, narcissism and impotence as a mirror in which America can see its own image.'[70]

Prevailing opinion shifted from worship of Pop to its disqualification, pure and simple. Buren, once adored by the theorists of the avant-garde and suspect in the eyes of the wider public on account his columns at the Palais Royal, and even more so after his collaboration with the Nina Ricci

---

70 Céna, 'Le blanc souci de rien', pp. 19ff.

71 Millet, 'Ce n'est qu'un début, l'art continue', p. 8.

fashion house, was abandoned by certain defenders of contemporary art.[71] Such reassessments, positive or negative, are par for the course in the history of art. If Minimalism wants to break with Abstract Expressionism, or Conceptual Art to challenge both Minimalism and Pop, these are the normal processes of development in both creation and critical reception. Within the overall history of art, such disputes do not lastingly undermine the status of the movements put into question. On the other hand, it is hardly sensible to utterly dismiss figures who have made their mark on this history, if only through controversy, and who have in any case the merit of having provoked movements in opposition.

Another point of attack: the affinity between modern art and science, chief source of the impoverishment that art is said to have suffered since the nineteenth century:

> The transitions from Impressionism to Cézanne, and then from Cézanne to Cubism (and on from Cubism to Abstraction) clearly demonstrate the successive losses entailed by the quasi-scientific researches of Modern Art.
>
> . . .
>
> Duchamp and Dadaism not only inspired André Breton and Surrealists such as Miró, Dali, Tanguy and Masson. With them emerged the curious idea, still with us, of the artistic avant-garde, that is to say, of movements that are ahead of the rest of the artistic work of a period, of cutting-edge theory, just indeed as there is cutting-edge scientific research. From having been influenced by science, and then fascinated by it, art has ended up, fatally, by identifying with it.[72]

---

72 Céna, 'Le blanc souci de rien', pp. 11, 15.

Not so long ago, the avant-gardes were criticized for their affinity with revolutionary movements; today, it is the influence of knowledge, the knowledge of primitive art, of psychoanalysis or of technology that is denounced—as if the art of the Renaissance, the art of the inventors of perspective, had been free of any scientific 'influence', as if expressive purity were in itself a guarantee of quality. The autonomy of art does not mean that art must confine itself to the sphere of expression and subjective experience. Its ambition has always extended beyond both experience and technique. Openness to the intellectual concerns of ones time has never meant 'identifying with science' or denying the specificity of art. The logic of aesthetic modernity entails precisely the sovereign appropriation of all possible contents, transformed into objects of experience and re-evaluated in terms of their expressive potential.

In this impasse between an officially sanctioned dogma and a reaction that hopes to escape the implications of a century or two of artistic discovery, all argument is vitiated from the start. Once art has lost its 'sacred' status, and rupture is not only managed but sought after by the institutions, the artist's authority can no longer be based on the tyrannous provocation of 'This is art, even if it disgusts you or leaves you cold.' An artistic statement now must rely not on a reinstated 'taste', always too easily offended by phenomena that fall outside the traditional definition of art, but on the possibility of justification, on the capacity to convince its audience of the pertinence of the choices made.

This idea runs counter to that of an historical succession of artistic innovations, whereby works are justified by the effects that they do in fact produce and the influence thus exerted on other artists. Historical succession is a purely factual and not an aesthetic (normative) criterion. It cannot be neglected, being of great importance to both artists and critics, but it is not a sufficient criterion, being incapable of distinguishing between artistic influence and general cultural, technical or other influences. Futurism was as 'influenced' by Cubism as by notable contemporary developments in technology, yet none of this speaks to the properly aesthetic interest of Futurist works.

A work may be historically 'important' without having the capacity to evoke an intense or profound aesthetic experience. A Duchamp ready-made does not have the same effect on us as a portrait by Francis Bacon: the experience it offers is primarily intellectual, provoking reflection on the mechanisms of the institution of art. Yet Duchamp's gesture inaugurated a whole series of other gestures of different kinds, which themselves may provoke aesthetic experiences, as for example Bertrand Lavier's *Mlle Goducheau,* which confronts us with the quasi-carceral nature of industrial work in its reduction of the person to the metal locker to be found in factory changing rooms.

The current debate on modern and contemporary art is in fact being driven and falsified by issues that go far beyond the sphere of art, touching as they do on the modern 'sensibility', on and openness to the unfamiliar experience that disturbs our perceptual and intellectual habits. The farewells to modernity, to the avant-gardes, to the experiences of post-War art in America and Europe, are often offered in bad faith: some who invested great hopes in art are engaged in a vast labour of disenchantment that denies their earlier engagement.[73] And in doing this they form fantastical alliances with those who never ever had any time for the radical experience of modernity. These two types of conservatism, the consistent and the turncoat—just as one finds in politics—join together in excluding from art any works that refuse an easy pleasure to the viewer.

---

[73] Notably Marc Le Bot and Jean Clair.

Defenders of contemporary art react to these critics as if they represented a resurgence of the old reaction that—from its mocking of Manet's *Olympia* to its endless denunciation of Duchamp's bottle-rack or urinal—has rejected the very idea of an art that breaks with the traditional principles of expression and representation. And it is true that most anti-contemporary polemics share a characteristic resentment: the denounced artists seem to have won a success not only undeserved but enormous; others, directly comparable in aesthetic terms, are spared on account of their more modest achievements.

Yet the unease provoked by contemporary art cannot be reduced to the resentments of yesteryear, and there are indeed at least two possible justifications for it. Firstly, the paradigm of the avant-garde, entailing a rejection of the new conditions of the art market, more particularly of the art object as commodity, and the wish to act directly on reality through art, the artwork being replaced by a labour of intervention—practically a political intervention—at the boundary between art and life, this paradigm is showing signs of exhaustion. Secondly, if questions of quality are again being raised and cannot be treated as simply reactionary, this is not only the result of a return to the 'work of art' in consequence of this exhaustion of the avant-gardist project of political intervention but also intimately connected to the paradoxes inherent in the management of contemporary art by public institutions.

The bankruptcy of avant-gardist neo-dogmatism is evident: it is the aesthetic of those who want to learn nothing, either about recent art or about the society that deserves it. The anti-avant-gardist reaction fails to comprehend the necessity of the aggression that is constitutive of contemporary art; it is furthermore incapable of understanding the links between art and science and truth and their social and political implications. To reduce art, in the name of a narrow interpretation of Kant, to the realm of sensation or self-expression, is to exclude from serious consideration those emphatic works that are the glory of twentieth-century art. Such a 'revisionism' leads only to a massive over-valuation of imitators of the art of the previous century.

towards an aesthetic logic

Goodman sought to separate the question of 'What is art' from the evaluative question 'What is good art?'[74] This positivist approach, inspired by the axiological neutrality of science, ignores the fact that the work of art or the aesthetic object inspire interest not for what they contribute to our knowledge of the world—on this terrain, science and documentary will always have the upper hand over art—but for the way in which they share certain symbolized values which they present and which create relations between those who perceive them. In the case of the work of art, as Kant showed, these are not purely personal.

If beauty, as Kant also says, is not an objective property of things, then the critic or the aesthetician cannot neutrally describe a work of art, ignoring its claim to aesthetic value. The only workable description is one that grasps the artwork in the light of its own artistic ambitions, and which seeks therefore to identify the nature of its coherence and intensity, its ambitions [*ses enjeux*]—what precisely is at stake in it—and its contemporary relevance for aesthetic experience. Without categories of this order, an object, a text, an image or a piece of music cannot be grasped *as* an aesthetic object or a work of art.

---

[74] Goodman, 'When Is Art?' in *Ways of Worldmaking*. See also my article, 'Logique cognitive et logique esthétique' in *Les Cahiers du Musée national d'art moderne 41: Nelson Goodman et les langages de l'art* (Autumn 1992), pp. 61–71.

In place of the demand for an 'autonomous' art, sensual and expressive, emptied of content and of socio-political implications, criticism should not turn to a general theory of symbols—this being no more, in fact, than a general theory of knowledge—but rely on independent aesthetic *criteria*. It is only in accordance with its own modalities that art—at the level of its ambitions, which are not purely artistic but also related to the general concerns of the period—*can* make a contribution to knowledge or to politics, a goal from which art has never shied away. Critics of art, music or literature will play a more modest role: they will no longer claim, together with the Romantics, Nietzsche or Benjamin, to challenge Western rationalism in the name of art, nor base a radical politics on the interpretation of avant-garde art. The critic will contribute to a public debate on the issues presented by the most eloquent works. S/he will act as the translator of a new way of seeing, of a critical awareness, identifying the issues concerning the values in play and their more or less successful formal embodiment by the artists.

A distinction drawn by the American pragmatist philosopher John Dewey may prove helpful here. He distinguishes between 'judicial' and 'impressionist' criticism, the first being eager to formulate a definitive verdict, while the second offers 'no unifying point of view'.[75] For Dewey, a number of different readings can be equally legitimate:

> The unity that the critic traces must be in the work of art
> as its characteristic. This statement does not signify that
> there is just one unifying idea or form in a work of art.
> There are many, in proportion to the richness of the
> object in question. What is meant is that the critic shall
> seize upon some strain or strand that is actually there,

---

75 John Dewey, *Art as Experience* (New York: G. P. Putnam's Sons, 1980 [1934]), p. 314.

and bring it forth with such clearness that the reader has a new clue and guide in his own experience . . . One mode of unification on the part of the critic is as legitimate as another—provided two conditions are fulfilled. One is that the theme and design which interest selects be really present in the work, and the other is the concrete exhibition of this supreme condition: the leading thesis must be shown to be consistently maintained throughout the parts of the work.[76]

It is thus impossible to describe a work of art without postulating a number of relations between its elements. These relations are not given, and to understand a work as an organized whole they must be constructed, grounded on both a hypothesis as to the meaning of the work and a wager on its ambition and its value. Unlike the aesthetic theorist, the critic is therefore always obliged to take sides. He cannot content himself with methodological premises; he must make choices that are not value-free.

Dewey also remarks that a simple verdict pronounced on a work of art has little significance; what constitutes true aesthetic judgement is the explicitation of the coherence and differentiation of its moments, a process through which the experience of the work can come to be more widely shared and more precisely situated within the field of possible aesthetic experiences.[77] 'The critic's moral function is exercised indirectly,'[78] not by approbation or condemnation but through the capacity to bring out the issues at stake and the means employed. Once the critic has suc-

---

76 Ibid.

77 Ibid., p. 310.

78 Ibid., p. 324

ceeded in so sharing a grounded experience of the work, he hardly needs to pronounce judgement.

In Friedrich Schlegel, the same idea takes on a different form, given the precise philosophical status of art in his system of thought: if a work were susceptible to critique, if its coherence could be reconstructed and amplified philosophically, then it was a success; otherwise, it merited destruction or silence. Here no further judgement is necessary because the creation of a work is the supreme act of thought, it is to speak what the philosophical understanding can merely hint at in a representation for which the thing in itself will be forever inaccessible. For Dewey, art is neither thought, nor true knowledge and so superior to philosophy: it is experience. His definition of aesthetic criticism is correspondingly liberal. Several different readings can be equally legitimate. But this tolerant attitude has no answer to the more difficult questions raised by works that are without any of the characteristics that have traditionally identified works of art.

PART TWO } **argumentation**

aesthetic rationality: between magic and reason

The way art is perceived is never innocent of presuppositions. It depends on visual habits and theoretical positions that guide, to a greater or lesser degree, the viewer's eye, privileging certain values and qualities and disparaging others, or drawing attention to hitherto unnoticed structures or details. Today, contemporary art's vision of itself, which also imbues the discourse on it, largely depends on critiques of modernity inspired by Nietzsche, Heidegger and Freud, and to some extent by Benjamin and Adorno. These are directed against Reason or discursive coherence, ascribing to art in general, and to the image more particularly, a central role in correcting discursive knowledge. In this, the image is seen as a configuration that escapes the grasp of the Western obsession with rational identity and certainty. One continues to talk about art—indeed, there has never been so much talk about it—but in doing so, to denounce speech and its privilege, 'the subjection of all the arts to speech'.[1] Thus it is that Jacques Derrida, for example, talks, in connection with Hegel and Heidegger, of the

---

1 Derrida, *The Truth in Painting*, p. 22. [Translation modified.]

'discursivity within the structure of the beautiful'.[2] Art, and more especially the art of the image, seems to confront us with a radically non-conceptual reality that traditional aesthetics has always reduced to discourse and reason.[3]

In more narrowly Freudian terms, Hubert Damisch notes that the aesthetic judgement 'goes in tandem with the repression for which it is the substitute'.[4] An aesthetics informed by psychoanalysis must look for the woman: 'Cherchez la femme!'[5]

> Where aesthetics are concerned . . . Kant, like the Greeks . . . *ne pensait qu'à ça*—despite all of the effort, all of the work of the third *Critique* in view of *displacing* the question of beauty, of uncoupling it from that of the 'charms' and substituting pure and disinterested pleasure for the more transient ones, to the point of replacing the euphemistic *ça* 'that' (that is, sex, the sexual drive) with the would-be speaking and judging subject.[6]

Kant himself, Damisch recalls, admits that 'apart from a reference to the subject's feeling, beauty is nothing by itself',[7] and concludes from this that

---

2 Ibid., p. 48.

3 In a similar way, Didi-Huberman denounces the logocentrism of the art historians: 'The history of art, a "modern" phenomenon par excellence—because born in the sixteenth century—has wanted to bury the ancient problematics of the *visual* and the *figurable* by giving new ends to artistic images, ends which place the visual under the tyranny of the *visible* (and of imitation), the figurable under the tyranny of the *legible* (and of iconology)' (Georges Didi-Huberman, *Confronting Images*, trans. John Goodman, University Park, PA: Penn State University Press, 2005, p. 8). 'The author thus opposes to the primacy of knowledge in art history the primcay of non-knowledge and desire' (ibid., pp. 51–2).

4 Hubert Damisch, *The Judgment of Paris* (Chicago: University of Chicago Press, 1996), p. 46.

5 Ibid., pp. 53–7.

6 Ibid., p. 57.

7 Immanuel Kant, *Critique of the Faculty of Judgment*, trans. Werner S. Pluhar (Indianapolis and Cambridge: Hackett Publishing Co., 1987), ss. 9, p. 63.

Kant is self-deconstructing: 'However dependent on verbal expression it is and must be, beauty, like pleasure, even when shared, is not a matter of consensus.'[8] It is the 'relation to feeling' or desire that must 'account for the judgement of taste in its most intimate manifestation, which is not intersubjective'.[9]

This argumentative strategy has usefully drawn attention to the irreducibility of the aesthetic. Nonetheless, it has difficulty in avoiding 'reasoning' about this 'other' of discourse that is the image. And as soon as it embarks on the analysis of a work, it finds itself confronted by intellectual articulations that only discourse can give an account of. What most intimately underpins the judgement of taste, this 'desire' that makes every art-lover a voyeur, is not what enables him to distinguish between Courbet's *Origin of the World* and a pornographic image. Nor does it allow him to say why the latter is not art. But if no feeling or desire can be significant from the aesthetic point of view, only the reasons that can be invoked to justify our admiration can make the difference. It can be admitted that the interest in art is motivated by desire—and not by 'cold reason'—without making it the single, monotonous key to aesthetic analysis. What ensures that analyses of Freudian inspiration remain prisoners to Kant is that they assume that there can be a pure aesthetic interest separable from all appreciation, all judgement, and hence also distinct from the reasons why we take pleasure in certain images and not in others. The (Kantian) question of whether judgement is anterior to aesthetic pleasure or vice versa is badly put, because there is hardly any 'primary' access to aesthetic pleasure. We realize this as soon as we see the photographic or painted representation of a pleasing object, a nude, fruit, flowers or a

---

8 Damisch, *The Judgment,* p. 45.

9 Ibid., pp. 44–5.

landscape, and our aesthetic 'conscience', or even quite simply our 'taste', 'censures' by a sense of frustration the immediate pleasure of the voyeurs that we are, reminding us of the difference between art and kitsch, and this not as the effect of repression but in the name of a pleasure sublimated by the intelligence. It is for the sake of its own satisfaction that aesthetic desire distances itself from its primitive inclinations.

For many, the reintroduction of a concept of 'aesthetic rationality', intended to free aesthetic experience both from its false philosophical pretensions and from a mystically inclined irrationalism, can only be seen as a worrying regression or an insignificant provocation. For them, the specificity of the image in particular, and of art more generally, as the subversion of 'Western reason' is unchallengeable. But it is precisely because the work of art does not obey the rules of discursive knowledge that it cannot enter into competition with it. Both have their logics and social functions, irreducibly distinct, which cannot in any way take each other's place. That such a replacement of 'Socratism' by tragedy, music or painting is both possible and desirable as a way of curing modernity of its destructive violence is the Nietzschean hope. Opposed to a substantial concept of Reason, the rehabilitated 'image' itself takes the form of a sublime and sacred substance, sometimes, as in Nietzsche or Adorno, of an underground counter-Reason. But such a status cannot be justified in terms of the aesthetic qualities either of sacred works or of the profane works of modernity.

It is a fact that one can well wonder what the point is of ratiocinating about art rather than loving or admiring it, creating or performing it, unaccompanied by any other form of discourse. But why do those who seek to preserve art from reason and discourse then talk so much about it? Art more readily provokes discussion than science or politics. But between this and any talk of 'rationality' is a step that seems to be deadly to both pleasure and what Nietzsche called the profound 'wisdom' of great art. Why not restrict oneself to lyrical or poetic tribute, to sober or enthusiastic celebration? Because works of art provoke differences of appreciation that are not gratuitous, and which, though they can but rarely be settled, nonetheless call for reasoned argument.

Art has always been the object of critiques and defences that put forward arguments for or against works under consideration. Why does contemporary art so often seem to be beyond the reach of criticism or rational justification? Why does the debate so often boil down to total rejection or blind solidarity? Oddly enough, this situation prevails both in the contemporary visual arts and, for example, in popular music. These domains seem to play, in the psychic economy of their partisans, the role of a radical refuge from the principles that govern today's world: economics, power, the functional sterility of everyday life. They seem to offer some of the rare spaces of freedom and uncompromising expression. To draw distinctions there seems to contaminate them with the perverse spirit of the rationalized world.

In the wake of a millennial disenchantment, art alone today seems capable of offering some semblance of the 'sacred' and of imposing a limit on an invasive reason. And fear in the face of modern autonomy tends primarily to find refuge in the quasi-religious attitude of the admirer and interpreter of canonical works. Judging and deciding for oneself should go without saying. In the political realm, whose structure depends on such autonomous judgement, this is challenged only by the anti-democratic instincts of nostalgics and profound sceptics. But the same principle also applies to the policies of art institutions, as soon as they claim to act in the public interest. If the judgement of every Tom, Dick or Harry seems to constitute a threat to the independence of artists and creators, if, as in the realm of science, the incompetence of the majority tends to inhibit innovation, rejecting anything that might challenge common sense and well-established prejudice, it is nonetheless indispensable that choices made in the name of all, should, in one way or another, be justified before all. Periodically, contemporary art becomes the subject of public debate on the 'abuse' represented by the challenges laid down by artists disinclined to compromise with the public, debates that invoke the common sense and the 'reasonableness' of the ordinary citizen. The role of 'aesthetic rationality' would be to remove the appearance of arbitrariness from the public recognition of works that at first sight are calculated to shock the sensibilities of a public unfamiliar with the language of contemporary art.

A legitimating reason, or a reason that interrogates legitimacy, becomes increasingly important with the growing enfeeblement of other mechanisms of regulation, such as the existence of a broad milieu of informed connoisseurs. The internal logic of a rationality is independent of its social function: when we speak of rationality in connection with questions of truth, justice or aesthetic quality, the concept refers not to a calculation independent of all perception, interpretation or appreciation, but to the 'normative dimension' that characterizes, in its different way each time, claims, acts or works.

To speak of aesthetic rationality is not a matter of provocatively rejecting a tradition that has made art the absolute other of the 'Socratic culture' and seeks jealously to protect it from all rational calculation. This tradition was not without legitimacy as a response to an undifferentiated extension of scientific rationalism and a puritan morality to the domain of the aesthetic. What is at issue here is something else. When one opposes art and reason, it is no longer possible to make distinctions between artworks and artistic events other than in the name of a particular sensibility or affinity, in the name of unjustified and unjustifiable preferences and complicities. And there may be very good reasons to distinguish between art and that which is not art, and to establish orders of importance within the different arts.

No rationality can predict or deduce an aesthetically significant work; aesthetic 'rationality' is not a matter of calculation, but of the reasons that enter into the decisions of artists; reasons which, however, as a general rule—and even in the case of Conceptual Art—can only be formulated after the event. Without endeavouring to reduce art as a whole to any form of reason, the notion of 'aesthetic rationality' is intended rather to identify a feature of works of art that distinguishes them from other objects, also themselves 'aesthetic', which is that they expect to be understood in their ambition and recognized for their success, such that they are susceptible of criticism and of reasoned justification. A distinction must be drawn between the status of a work of art as a non-discursive configuration and the rationality that gives the measure of its achievement and its appreciation. A natural phenomenon cannot be criticized in the same way, because it makes no claim of its own to aesthetic value. Such value is only attributed to it from without, and if such a phenomenon is said to be beautiful or ugly then it is only this claim, not the thing itself, that can be criticized. A work of art, on the other hand, always presents itself as being worthy of attention by virtue of certain qualities. Even an object deliberately made almost imperceptible lays claim to this critical attention in presupposing the normally perceptible character of a work that is intended to be recognized as such.

Benjamin discusses artistic phenomena that a community addresses exclusively to God or to magical forces:

The elk portrayed by the man of the Stone Age on the walls of his cave was an instrument of magic. He did expose it to his fellow men, but in the main it was meant for the spirits. Today the cult value would seem to demand that the work of art remain hidden. Certain statues of gods are accessible only to the priest in the cella; certain Madonnas remain covered nearly all year round; certain sculptures on medieval cathedrals are invisible to the spectator on ground level.[10]

But he adds that, 'With the emancipation of the various art practices from ritual go increasing opportunities for the exhibition of their products.'[11] Benjamin concludes from this to the disappearance of the aesthetic function associated with ritual, replaced by other functions, notably political. One might more relevantly deduce that the aesthetic function itself only becomes general with the exhibition or presentation of the work to a virtually universal public. It is then that it truly stakes its claim to attention, until then directed only to a single addressee so as to achieve non-aesthetic, instrumental ends related to the material or spiritual well-being of the community.

The notion of rationality always refers to a form of knowledge, whether intellectual or practical. The minimal rationality required of the beholder of a work of art is to know how to distinguish between aesthetic 'unreality' and empirical reality, which implies a break with mythical or magical behaviours.[12] So long as there is confusion between art and the sacred, the work of art is not seen as such, being only the sublime 'symptom' of an event that transcends it. The assimilation of art to ethics in a committed

---

10 Benjamin, 'The Work of Art . . .', in *Illuminations*, p. 218.

11 Ibid., pp. 218–19.

12 Danto, *The Transfiguration of the Commonplace*, p. 77: 'The concept of art was itself undergoing a transformation, or rather, was only beginning to be formed there [in Greece], for

art (be the commitment moral, religious, social or political) can also present quasi-magical features in the desire to influence or indoctrinate that abolishes the aesthetic suspension of discursive or practical constraints. What is presented to us for our reflection may act but indirectly on our convictions.

Danto even wonders whether art—in the sense of a production no longer associated with magical or religious rites—is not connected, from its historical beginnings, with the emergence of the philosophical concept of reason, to the capacity to distinguish between being and representation:

> Under the structures of magic, these figures and rites had no semantic structure; they only acquired that when they began to be representations in the sense of standing for what it was also believed they resembled. And then, over time, standing for or denoting came to be less and less an important thing for artworks to do, except in special commemorative cases, portraits, historical paintings and the like.[13]

In Greece, Danto continues, in the very age in which philosophy was born, 'images were seen as contrasting with a reality they had previously been supposed to participate in.'[14] Since Nietzsche, art's radical loss of the magical character proper to mimesis—and hence the rationality of art—has been ceaselessly challenged. For Adorno, works of art, despite their rational character and their irreducible break with magic, are modern echoes of 'the

---

what preceded it would have been less a concept of art than a concept of magic . . . This semantic relationship [between art and world] probably dawned at the very dawn of philosophy itself. Though there was art in Egypt and Mesopotamia and elsewhere, it is not clear that it was seen as what we today would call art—representations in the semantic rather than in the magical sense of the word.'

13 Ibid.

14 Ibid.

primordial shudder'.[15] In their character as appearance, deliberately presented as unreal and thus itself 'rational', there survives a portion of magic that implicitly denounces the violence inherent in all reason.

The idea of an 'aesthetic rationality' was late in emerging and is far from being unchallenged. The temptation to restore a metaphysical or religious function to art remains strong, given that the artwork has several features it shares with the cult object: to gain access to it, the rules of everyday life must be suspended, while the distanced attention that it evokes also relates it to such an object of cultic focus. And deliberate damage to a unique work of art is as fiercely condemned as sacrilege.

rationality and sovereignty

When in recent debates art has been presented as the subversion of non-aesthetic reason, one might ask what reason precisely is being put into question: is it only philosophical reason—and more particularly that which dogmatically asserts the rationality of the real—or is it rather ordinary reason and common sense as employed by all of us in everyday life? Should aesthetic subversion concern *all* reason, one is left to ask what might be the function and consequences of such a disqualification of reason in the name of signs irreducible to determinate meaning. The everyday use of reason either tremains untouched by this subversion, happily coexisting with it, or—in the most radical conceptions—is shaken to its foundations by art.

In the tradition of aesthetic theory, an important step was taken in the late eighteenth century, when, with Shaftesbury and Diderot, Kant and the Jena Romantics, the sphere of the aesthetic was distinguished from that of

---

15 Adorno, *Aesthetic Theory*, p. 79.

knowledge and morality. It would henceforth be concerned with reflective judgement, or, in the Romantic theory of the artwork, with immanent interpretation that presupposes no pre-established rule. But at the same time, and in consequence, it seems to be grounded in the pure genius of the creator and to be inaccessible to any specific rationality. The ambiguity of these theories opened the door either to an irrationalism that made the aesthetic sphere the radical other of reason, or to a new dogmatic rationalism that subordinated the criteria of aesthetic value to implicitly heterogeneous demands, whether religious, ideological or intellectual. Since that time, aesthetic theory has been marked by a duality between theories that posit the absolute 'irreducibility' of the phenomenon of art and those that consider it to be the repository of a reason and a truth 'superior' to those of rational knowledge.[16] The former claim that art escapes all forms of rationality, the latter hold that it is the guarantee of true rationality or of reason at all. From the first, then, autonomy and sovereignty have been closely connected. Since the emergence of theories of aesthetic autonomy, the tendency to replace a defective philosophical reason by poetical or aesthetic reason has always been present.

Alongside a 'Romantic' conception of sovereignty, some have identified in Adorno and Derrida a 'Modern' conception, based not on a higher knowledge embodied in art but on the subversive structure of the work of art, whose meaning can never be definitively pinned down, and on the omnipresent possibility of the emergence within communication of a destabilization of hermeneutic dogmatism and its conviction that understanding is always possible.[17] Sovereignty would reside, then, in the autonomy of the

---

16 See Martin Seel, *Die Kunst der Entzweiung*: *zum Begriff der ästhetischen Rationalitat* (Frankfurt am Main: Suhrkampf, 1985).

17 Christoph Menke, *The Sovereignty of Art*: *Aesthetic Negativity in Adorno and Derrida*, trans. Neil Solomon (Cambridge, MA and London: MIT Press, 1998).

work of art's 'letter' from its 'spirit'. In amplifying this subversive potential of the work of art, aesthetic critique seems to extend the sovereignty of the work beyond the aesthetic sphere in the strict sense. Yet reduced to a source of hermeneutic disquiet, the sovereignty of art loses both the character of superior knowledge suggested by aesthetic theories since Romanticism and any positive sense of the opening of new horizons capable of being formulated in terms of well-defined theoretical positions. Criticism, for its part, will inevitably reduce the destabilizing power of the work by privileging a determinate interpretation and serving as a mediation between the work and non-aesthetic communication.

If one assumes, on the other hand, that aesthetic subversion is hardly capable of any effect on everyday reason as a whole, having no purchase on it in so far as it takes place only in the non-quotidian domains of social life, then one can propose another concept of the sovereignty of art that relates in a different way to its autonomy. Goodman and Danto have shown the unlimited character of the faculty of aesthetic symbolization, any object and any sign being potentially subject to aesthetic derealization, a potential particularly evident in modern art since the beginning of the twentieth century. With Cubism and the readymade, art's annexation of objects of every kind has seen it exercise a sovereignty hitherto unparalleled. Within an exhibition space—but only in a domain previously defined as appertaining to art—one may today expect to see the aesthetic derealization of any and every kind of seemingly everyday useful objects.

But such an exercise of 'sovereignty', itself undermined by the abandonment of its pretensions in the face of the 'reality' of the objects, has its limits. When in an art gallery those attending an opening, having left their coats at the entrance, enter a room that could not be more empty, only to learn later that the coat-racks at the entrance were supposed to be the art, the derealization has not been effected for the lack of a space defined as related to art. To be a work of art, an object must sooner or later be presented as a work and must be capable of being recognized as such, which equally implies the possibility of refusing it the name. A cleaning-lady would not be completely wrong in throwing away a dirty rag, even if the artist who cleaned his brushes on it had earlier made it a work; such an object has a priori nothing of art about it if it is not explicitly presented as a candidate for the title of artwork and isolated from the real from which it has been taken in order to be derealized within an artistic configuration. And in an exhibition too, nothing obliges us to accept the artist's claim to 'open our eyes' with objects of this kind. If one decides that art is a priori defined by a declaration of intent, the public reclaims its right of judgement in turning away with indifference and returning to classic works that display more easily identifiable artistic characteristics. Repeated without substantial innovation, the gestures of non-art do not satisfy one of our requirements of a work of art: that it should surprise us by offering a novel perspective; the rejection of the criterion of originality commonly applied in traditional art cannot here be invoked, given that this type of intervention derives its aesthetic legitimacy only from the effect of surprising derealization.

Jorge Luis Borges's tale of Pierre Menard is very like a thought experiment. Identical reproduction in a different context does not necessarily make another work of the work, but—like a critique of a work in the light of its successors—at the very most another interpretation of the same work. Danto argues:

> Works are in part constituted by their location in the history of literature as well as by their relationship to their authors, and as these are often dismissed by critics who urge us to pay attention to the work itself, Borges' contribution to the ontology of art is stupendous: you cannot isolate these factors from the work since they

> penetrate, so to speak, the *essence* of the work. And so, graphic
> congruities notwithstanding, these are deeply different works.[18]

And it is true that place in history and relationship to the author are not extraneous to the 'constitution' of artworks, with the result that, in theory, two perfectly identical texts can have different meanings. In practice, however, such examples have only demonstrative value. They do indeed show that the identity of a work is not only a question of its symbolic materiality, but not that Pierre Menard's work, imagined by Borges—unlike Borges's fiction itself—is worthy of interest. It is in a determinate context of twentieth-century art that such experiments and such games with indistinguishable doubles have exercised a certain fascination as a subversion of the myth of the unique original with its meaning defined once and for all. This fascination is not inexhaustible, but it is not for aesthetics to offer an authoritative judgement on the matter.

Danto himself displays a revealing ambivalence. On the one hand, his tolerance for the extension of the concept of art seems to be limitless: 'anything could be art.'[19] On the other, he speaks only with irony of those modern works that are simple replicas of real objects:[20] it's just that he can't see any logical reason to exclude them from art. He reproaches the authors of a catalogue of pedagogical drawings and doodles by Beuys for treating these drawings 'as if they were art in an earlier sense which Beuys did so much to alter',[21] comparing them to the works of Leonardo, Dürer, Klee

---

18 Danto, *The Transfiguration of the Commonplace*, p. 36.

19 Arthur C. Danto, 'Four-and-twenty Blackboards: Drawing and Thinking in the Work of Joseph Beuys', *Times Literary Supplement* (17 December 1993), p. 17.

20 See Danto's discussion of the imaginary artist 'J.' in *The Transfiguration of the Commonplace*, pp. 2ff., 28–9 and elsewhere.

21 Danto, 'Four-and-twenty Blackboards', p. 17.

and Munch. There remains only to formulate a well-grounded argument, free of conservative prejudice, that would allow one to distinguish conceptually between 'art in the old sense' and 'art in the post-historical sense': but such an argument, which would amount to the reintroduction in disguise of the distinction between art and non-art, has not yet been proffered by Danto.

The sovereignty of art has its limits, as Bataille underlined in the questions he asked himself about Genet.[22] These concerned, notwithstanding a certain irresponsibility intrinsic to art as the suspension of everyday rules and obligations, the concept of the artist's responsibility. The artist, it is true, obeys only those rules he imposes on himself; it must nonetheless be possible to reconstruct these and to evaluate their relevance, interest, scope and fruitfulness—criteria that mobilize a certain 'aesthetic rationality'. Inversely, to have the right to judge, the viewer when embarking on the experience of the work must start off from a position of 'prejudice in favour of success'. For both creator and viewer, the work represents a demand, and excessive indulgence can only lead to narcissism in the former and indifference in the latter.

The phrase 'aesthetic rationality' denotes a form of rationality applicable only to aesthetic value. In certain respects, it is analogous to truth and falsity in the domain of knowledge and to normative justice in the domain of ethics, but it is irreducible to these types of validity. For one can

---

22 Georges Bataille, *Literature and Evil*, trans. Alastair Hamilton (London: Marion Boyars, 1973), p. 192: 'To produce a work of literature is to turn ones back on servility, as on every conceivable form of diminution. It is to talk the sovereign tongue which, coming from that sovereign part of man, is addressed to sovereign humanity . . . Genet's work as a writer is worthy of attention. Genet himself is eager to be sovereign. But he has not seen that sovereignty calls for an impulse of the heart, for faithfulness to ones commitments, because it arises in communication.' [Translation of second part of last sentence modified.]

contest the value of a work of art despite its being logically or morally irreproachable; and one can defend it though it might be absurd or immoral, even as a theory can be valid without being elegant.

Aesthetic rationality becomes manifest through specific arguments on the qualities of works of art, notably through the challenges to which they have been subject and the justifications in response. Unlike natural or cultural objects without artistic pretensions, works of art are designed to stand up to precisely this kind of contestation, having survived the critical examination of the artist's own eye. Despite certain Romantic theories that present the artist as an insensate creature or irrational genius, aesthetic rationality is no stranger to him; he presents to the public only what is sufficiently solid and coherent to 'satisfy' its demands, even if he should rebuff its expectations through innovation. Conversely, nothing can be considered a work of art worthy of the name that cannot be defended against certain specific challenges. Apart from certain very general rules, every age defines the standards for what it is prepared to consider artistically significant, norms that cannot be arbitrarily set aside but can only be purposefully transgressed.

Unlike a natural spectacle, every work of art is the fruit of an operation which if not necessarily calculated is at least accomplished—or, in the case of automatic writing, selected—with a certain goal in mind. This operation, which can always fail, demands recognition of its success. The work is made available to the public only when its creator or creators believe that it can withstand the critical gaze, and that it is worthy of its attention by virtue of a certain significance. It is this intersubjectivity of a recognition that is both sought and—in the case of success—gained to varying degrees, that is here designated by the term 'aesthetic rationality'. A work is successful if it is possible to put forward good reasons to justify the artistic qualities that are attributed to it. A work fails if in its realization it falls short of its ambitions and cannot be justified by convincing reasons.

Whatever degree of universality might be attained by such recognition, it seems evident that the private satisfaction of a person—whether the artist himself or a public reduced to no more than a single enthusiast—is not enough to constitute an aesthetic relationship such as is proper to art. In the case of nature, the aesthetic effect is contingent and unintended. Even if I am capable of indicating the reasons why a particular natural spectacle enchants me or otherwise impresses me aesthetically, there is here— without presupposing a religious relationship to Creation that cannot be demanded of everyone—no intersubjective context of recognition (the landscape claims nothing and awaits no judgement) and hence no 'aesthetic rationality'. For a work to be recognized as such, and thus be at least partially successful, it is not enough for someone to experience pleasure before it and to say, 'I like that.' That would be a judgement of pleasure, but not a considered judgement of art. As Kant emphasizes, to say that a work is 'beautiful' (artistically successful) is not to say that it is 'beautiful *for me*'.[23] I consider myself to have reasons of a certain type for making the judgement, though they might not allow one to formulate a doctrine on the basis of which it would be possible to create successful works. One must therefore distinguish from this requirement of rationality any aesthetic relation to things or beings based on an experience of pleasure or preference without 'normative' implication.

Any supposed work of art whose artistic quality cannot be justified by a good reason is not one. Anything at all, of course, can always be justified in the name of one reason or another; and many artefacts claiming the status of art find defenders ready to invoke reasons to legitimize them. But not every work succeeds in attracting a cluster of convincing justifications nor in evoking the practical attention of other artists, grounded in implicit

---

23 Immanuel Kant, *Critique of Judgment* (New York: Barnes and Noble, 2005), ss. 7, p. 55.

arguments, which draws it into a debate engaging the history of art. It is this demand inherent in every work of art worthy of the name that confers upon it a 'normative' value.

It is in this sense that, contrary to the claims of theorists like Nelson Goodman, it is not a matter of indifference whether a work of art is good or bad. If it is radically inadequate, and if this inadequacy can be pertinently explained, it cannot belong to the sphere of art, but is rather to be considered a school exercise, amateurism, the fabrication of a useful object, a leisure activity such as DIY, etc. We do not speak of a 'work of art' when a child makes a pretty or amusing drawing, or composes a poem that rhymes more or less correctly, no more than we speak in earnest when we say of an elaborate wedding cake, for example, that it is 'a real work of art'.

The explicit intention of the creator is not decisive. It matters not whether an artist deliberately intended to produce a work; in rare cases, a work may be recognized as such without its maker ever having claimed such recognition, in such a case most often understanding himself as a simple craftsman, though one whose vision transforms his product. Inversely, whatever might be the claim of certain avant-gardists to authoritatively determine what is or is not art, the intention to make an artwork is not a criterion of art, or of artistic quality, any more than the intention to tell the truth guarantees the reliability of a statement. A text may be literary rather than scientific or administrative—it can even have artistic ambitions—without its being a work of art,[24] for its failure to satisfy certain demanding criteria that we associate with this title if we want to be taken seriously.

---

24 See Gérard Genette, *Fiction and Diction,* trans. Catherine Porter (Ithaca and London: Cornell University Press, 1993), p. 20, which defends the contrary position: 'a given sonnet, good, bad, or indifferent is a literary work. The constitutional literariness of works of fiction or poetry—like the equally constitutive "artisticness" of most of the other arts—is in some sense, within the limits of the cultural history of humanity, inalienable and independent of any eval-

the limits of aesthetic rationality

A challenge to the traditional notion of art is central to many of the most characteristic artistic productions of the twentieth century, and such acts of self-authorization have led many theoreticians to grant the artist the exclusive right and capacity to determine what a work of art can and must be. The repetition of such gestures does however raise the problem of knowing if, given the inaugural radicalism of earlier initiatives, such pretensions are legitimate when subsequent endeavours introduce no new reflection on the status of the work of art. It must in any event be possible to recognize the artistic character of an act of presentation that is otherwise in principle within the power of anyone.

Goodman suggested that the essentialist question 'What is art?' be abandoned in favour of the conditional question, 'When is art?'[25] It would in this way be possible to count as works of art non-art objects that 'function as a work of art at some times and not at others'.[26] There remains however the question of *what* there is *when* one claims that there is art. This dimension escapes the merely descriptive: the fact of deploying or finding oneself confronted with a particular type of symbol (as in exemplification, even metaphoric) does not at all imply that the phenomenon in question has the status of a work of art, or even pretends to it. Goodman replaces aesthetic rationality with an undifferentiated cognitive rationality that leaves aside the phenomenon of the work of art and its normative demand: to be recognized under certain criteria of success. His nominalist demystification of essentialism provides no criteria capable of

---

uation.' Or p. 40 (note): 'As Nelson Goodman comes close to saying, if all bad works are excluded from the field of art, the risk is that there will be very little left, for the vast majority of works of art . . . are bad ones, which by no means keeps them from being works of art.'

25 Goodman, 'When Is Art?' in *Ways of Worldmaking*, pp. 57–70.

26 Ibid., p. 66.

guaranteeing that what in certain conditions ('when . . . ') is considered to be art is so considered for good reasons.

A pertinent critique of Goodman must thus show that the criteria by virtue of which the title of work of art is attributed are not essentialist but are connected with a procedure of aesthetic argumentation. In so far as Goodman envisages an isolated subject declaring that a given object is now considered to be art, he is only replacing essentialist arbitrariness with another form of rigidity, that of a subjective and authoritarian declaration such as is characteristic of certain avant-gardist dogmatisms, or again, conventional criteria based, for example, on the frequency of exemplification or of the representation of affect in art; but Goodman is prudent enough to admit that these modes of symbolization are also employed for non-artistic ends (e.g. in the provision of commercial samples or in the dramaturgy of everyday life).

From the point of view of aesthetic experience, in creation or enjoyment, it may be objected to the concept of 'aesthetic rationality' that art is first of all a matter of sensibility, or of pre-logical, irrational and a-rational faculties more generally. How, without violence, does one 'rationalize' the 'touch' of a painter of pianist, the 'tone' of a writer or composer, the idiosyncratic qualities of each artist? It is not a question of rationalizing what is not rational but if it is impossible to distinguish this kind of *je ne sais quoi* from other less moving or less convincing offerings, it is difficult to see what gives it its artistic character. And what is more, there is no art that consists of nothing but such ungraspable features. Touch and tone are always the product of a more complex and more precisely analysable structure whose own characteristics they unfold. The most sublime touch will not make an artwork of a sonata that has no existence in terms of technique and musical imagination; the most subtle or most vigorous touch of a painter cannot make up for the absence of an idea.

The concept of aesthetic rationality seems inadequate, finally, and above all, to the 'ultimate' dimension of art, to its 'mystery', its metaphysical or religious content. What rationality could account for the profundity of great works of music, visual art or literature? But perhaps this is indeed a matter of their aesthetic rationality. Works of art have no other language than that in which they appear to us, whose analysable organization is the only source of the emotion they provoke. An inarticulate mystery is no more than an obscure feeling and, if there is a way of approaching the mystery, it can only be through the elucidation and justification of what one perceives and what one experiences, of what one can understand and analyse.

If art has the sovereign power to annexe any reality capable of presentation, it exercises this through the suspension of other forms of rationality.[27] When we produce, admire or judge a work of art, we take account of a number of criteria that can be reconstructed. Unlike a flower, or a storm, a work of art—just like a sentence, an act, a symbolic or bodily gesture towards another—lays claim to a certain type of validity: it intends to be understood, and it can be criticized. But unlike a claim to cognitive truth or normative legitimacy, the claim to aesthetic validity is indirect: before assenting or dissenting, we must suspend judgement and enter into the play of a work that imposes a derealization, distancing us from our everyday attitudes. When we are offered an appreciation or interpretation of a work of art, these in turn can be validated only by an experience of the work in the light of these 'guides to reading'. Before judging a theory or

---

27 It is this that Coleridge refers to in speaking of the 'suspension of disbelief' by the reader of a tale; and one might add to this the suspension of the moral obligations he feels towards others in real life. 'Nothing is sacred to the poet,' writes Diderot, 'not even virtue, which he will heap with scorn, if the character and the moment require it . . . Does he introduce an evil character? You find that character odious' (Denis Diderot, *Oeuvres esthétiques*, Paris: Garnier, 1968, p. 252).

a philosophy too we have in a way to take in the entirety of the ideas and propositions in which it is formulated, but there we never leave the sphere of argument. Each proposition can be individually contested, which is never the case for a work of art, each element of which can be justified by the place it has in the whole. This is why the coherence of a work of art—the 'responsibility' of each detail taken separately having been suspended—is here more decisive, although less logically rigorous, than in the case of the logical coherence of a discourse or the normative coherence of a series of acts; less rigorous, because most often there are several legitimate possibilities for relating the elements.

The listener or viewer has to be capable of distinguishing between a fortuitous aesthetic effect and a structurally aesthetic signification, even if the aesthetic pleasure may be the same in both cases: natural beauty and artistic beauty are in this respect distinct aesthetic objects: before interpretation, natural beauty symbolizes nothing. For Goodman, the intellectual satisfaction of the theorist, the disinterested character of research, the absence of immediate practical goals, etc. evidence an affinity between art and science.[28] Conversely, according to the same Goodman, 'to be aesthetic does not stop something being unsatisfactory',[29] so much so that it seems impossible to establish a line of demarcation between art and other cognitive activities. But science remains scientific even if it is (aesthetically) unsatisfactory. Furthermore, the 'disinterestedness' of science, invoked by analogy with that of art, does not have the same meaning. All scientific knowledge, even 'fundamental research', adopts to reality an objectifying attitude susceptible of translation into technical mastery; in this sense, the

---

28 Goodman, *Languages of Art*, pp. 284–309. See also my essay 'Logique cognitive et logique esthétique', *Les Cahiers du Musée national d'art moderne* 41 (1992), pp. 61–71.

29 Goodman, *Languages of Art*, p. 286.

endeavour to identify a virus is not disinterested and may logically serve to produce a vaccine. In contrast, even a utilitarian object transformed into a work of art, like Duchamp's urinal, is addressed to no functional 'interest'. Conversely, that which is technically and radically unsatisfactory from the artistic point of view—in the type of symbols employed, the absence of exemplarity, or by virtue of other criteria—all the while susceptible to aesthetic 'perception', can cease to be considered as a work of art.

For every period, to understand a work of art one has to be familiar with a certain number of historical conditions of artistic creation if one is to be in a position to grasp the issues at stake in a work. As is emphasized by both Wölfflin and Danto, 'not everything is possible at every time.'[30] Aesthetic rationality includes knowledge about what can be art—or what art can be—given its recent past and the possibilities that it holds. No 'aesthetic rationality' would have enabled one to defend, in 1800, the artistic character of the readymade or the Minimalist cube, while a canvas painted today, comparable in facture and technique to Delacroix's *Massacre at Chios* and without any further sophistication (e.g in the manner of Sherry Levine), would be seen as a copy or as an academic exercise and not as a work capable of responding to the current preoccupations of art.

---

30 Danto, *The Transfiguration of the Commonplace*, p. 113.

symbol and symptom:
language for one, language for all

Compromised by its idealist connotations and the relativization that seemingly followed from its counterposition to allegory, after Cassirer the symbol found itself reintroduced into aesthetics in a more general and more neutral form, notably by Goodman. This promising approach allowed a nuanced analysis of modes of symbolization and hence also of what distinguishes the artistic from the cognitive symbol. Like structuralist semiology, Goodman frees reflection on art from the arbitrary character of approaches based on such unverifiable notions as spirit, emotion and sensation. And like structuralist semiology, he addresses himself primarily to knowledge, unlike poststructuralist criticism that emphasizes rather the energetic aspect of art, its subversion of all constituted knowledge and social conventions.

The Goodmanian concept of symptom is not opposed to that of symbol, art as symptom even offering a 'clue' to aesthetic symbolization.[31] For every work of art makes use of a 'symbolic medium' in the broad sense, systems of signs. However, the status of the artistic symbol and what

---

31 Goodman, *Ways of Worldmaking*, p. 68.

distinguishes it from other types of symbols, those of science, media and law, does not seem sufficiently defined only by the 'characteristics' or 'symptoms' of syntactic and semantic density, saturation of the signifier, exemplification of the whole by reference to its parts, and multiple and complex reference,[32] none of which is specific to art. Without claiming to formulate 'a crisp criterion',[33] it may be possible to more clearly delimit what differentiates the artistic symbol and by so doing afford an escape from the debate between a metaphysical or positivist cognitivism on the one hand, and an aesthetic irrationalism that rejects any attempt to justify its criteria of preference on the other.

The subversion of reason has itself become an exercise rationally organized by literary, musical and artistic institutions. In such a context, artistic activity is conceived as the production not so much of symbols as of symptoms, in a stronger sense of the word. Perhaps no work of art worthy of the name is constituted of neutral symbols as used by everyone; a sub-jective experience (Gr. *pathos*) that presses towards symbolization in an unprecedented language, sometimes strange, even alien, underlies all artistic objectivation. But the presentation of symptoms alone falls short of art, and the analysis of symptoms falls short of aesthetics.[34] The disman-tling of aesthetic idealism has brought with it a confusion of categories.

Artistic activity elaborates materials, translating experiences and mak-ing them possible through a symbolic structure whose apprehension con-stitutes the comprehension and recognition of the work. This elaboration

---

32 Ibid.

33 Goodman, *Languages of Art,* p. 252.

34 De Duve (in 'Ryman irreproductible', *Essais datés 1*, p. 137, n. 15) correctly observes that 'cer-tain art critics—some of the best among them—. . . refuse to declare their judgments of quality (but not to make them, which would be impossible) and . . . are inevitably led to treat the domain of art as if it were nothing but the privileged terrain of a general cultural symptomatology.'

tends to accentuate the singularity of the artist's point of view, being its stylization under the auspices of a certain logic. It involves making a singular experience necessary, without transcending it towards another order of necessity (of truth or of conformity to norms).

The structure elaborated may indeed make manifest an individual or collective attitude, but it is not from *this* point of view that it can be seen as the work of an artist aiming for aesthetic achievement. Otherwise it is only a symptom, an object of scientific decipherment by a competent observer. The symptom evokes a 'deep interpretation',[35] in other words an explanation that 'would not be a reason for him whose action it explains if it were conscious'.[36] In other words, it is not through deep interpretation that the work of the artist can itself be recognized; such an interpretation can only be a pretext for more general considerations that it serves to illustrate.

Unlike the symptom, connected to what it reveals by links of cause and effect, the symbol is not the unintended effect of an experience undergone. It signifies of itself, autonomously; in other words, it has no need of indirect explanation by causal or motivational hypotheses. This does not mean that the artistic symbol symbolizes only what the artist deliberately intended it to signify;[37] to be able to produce an aesthetic coherence and to translate it in terms of theory or interpretation are two different things. The artist produces a system of signs referring primarily to each other and forming a

---

35 See Danto, 'Deep Interpretation' in *The Philosophical Disenfranchisement of Art*, pp. 47–67.

36 Ibid., p. 52.

37 Despite what Danto claims ('The Appreciation and Interpretation of Works of Art' in *The Philosophical Disenfranchisement of Art*, p. 44): 'I believe we cannot be deeply wrong if we suppose that the correct interpretation of object-as-artwork is the one which coincides most closely with the artist's own interpretation.' Danto arrives at this position because he identifies the meaning of a work with the 'theory' on the basis of which the artist has produced it: 'To see something as art at all demands nothing less than this, an atmosphere of artistic theory, a knowledge of the history of art' (Danto, *The Transfiguration of the Commonplace*, p. 134).

coherent whole in which the artist recognizes the translation of the experience that he is concerned to symbolize. But he can hardly foresee all the implications, all the potentialities, all the interpretations and all the possible applications of the schema he has produced. Yet those applications that escape him are not susceptible of symptomatic explanation.

Contrary to what is suggested by the concept of intention, the creator of an artistic symbol cannot at all control its possible translations and interpretations. Even in the case of everyday symbolic expression of the referential type, without the least artistic ambition, meaning and intention are two different things. If I give someone information about the state of health of a third party, what I say and my intention in saying it require two distinct acts of comprehension. It may be that my communication is intended only to provoke my interlocutor to reveal his professional ambitions, or contrariwise to demonstrate his loyalty; without affecting the meaning of the statement, my intentions might escape my control, revealing, for instance, a pathological distrust.

In the case of the artistic symbol, the absence of an identifiable referent introduces a further gap between meaning and intention. A symbol of this kind signifies precisely in the absence of any information about the intentions of its author. This is what distinguishes in principle a literary work from an informational communication, or a pictorial work from an illustration in a handbook.

The artistic symbol does not 'denote', either directly or by exemplification or reverse reference.[38] Otherwise, its significance could be communicated independently of the artistic medium. If the colour grey referred to the predicate 'sad', which in turn 'denotes' it,[39] aesthetic 'knowledge'

---

38 Goodman, *Languages of Art*, pp. 84–6.

39 Ibid., pp. 85ff.

would be no more than a tiresome detour. What is evoked by the symbolic scheme of a work of art—without its being open to arbitrary interpretation—is precisely never so determinate; furthermore, even Goodman admits that 'we may hesitate to say that a sample refers to one rather than another among alternative predicates.'[40] The sense (the supposed referent) of the denotative signification is unstable and subject to ever-renewed interpretation. What constitutes the work as such is not this, but the realization of a successful and significant aesthetic coherence that remains open to different readings.

Stripped by definition of all reference, the artistic symbol relates first of all to the 'language' that it constitutes and within which it takes on meaning. This does not have the structure of a linguistic system or language constituted by a series of differences, abstract and general,[41] but of an utterance or text with its own rules and distinct rhythms. This is why an approach modelled on linguistics can only serve as an auxiliary science to aesthetics; the singular phenomenon with its own rules will escape it by reason of its very method.

The very first stroke of a drawing, a composition, a literary text, the first choice of a medium, material or object, already belong to a language, to a way of signifying, and not to a pre-symbolic reality. It is within symbolic structures that cognitive claims, moral and legal obligations to others, and artistic expressions, evaluations or configurations are distinguished from each other.

Though the work of art represents the end point of a process, it is not its completion that marks its accession to the level of the artistic symbol:

---

40 Ibid., p. 88.

41 Ferdinand de Saussure, *Course in General Linguistics*, Charles Bally and Albert Sechehaye (eds), trans. Roy Harris (London: Duckworth, 1983), p. 118.

this terminal moment determines only the degree of success. Numerous intermediary stages are possible definitive works and, as such, achieved artistic symbols.[42] What distinguishes these different symbolizations from each other is rather the breadth of scope they achieve in their transformation from idiosyncratic experience to intersubjectively significant experience. The object of artistic work is the stylization or manifestation of singularity in its most generally significant aspects, and what characterizes such artistic stylization, in even its most universal forms, is in every case the persistence of an irreducibly singular element. The most abstract of forms accede to the realm of art only by virtue of their individualization and their ability to touch individuals in their intimate experience. In this sense, the work of art is the intersubjective sharing of a 'subjective world', a publication of the private. The problem of aesthetic theory is to explain the nature of a symbol—intersubjective and universally intelligible by definition—that is supposed to conserve the characteristics of singular experience, being universal only by virtue of this singularity.

Compared to the universality of language, the poem is the most eloquent illustration of this paradox. Neither in the visual arts nor in music is there a codified symbolism comparable to language. The poem is singular in the very use it makes of language—an utterance [*parole*] indeducible from language [*langue*], to the point of being untranslatable in consequence of the fusion of sound and meaning that it effects—yet intelligible independently of any immediate context of communication. Unlike a letter, a poem claims to provide all the signification necessary to its comprehension, without need for any appeal to external information

---

42 See, for example, the successive states of Matisse's *Rêve* or *Blouse roumaine* in *Oeuvres de Matisse*, Collections du Musée d'art moderne (Paris: Éditions du Centre Pompidou, 1979), pp. 65–9, 76–9.

about its author, her acquaintanceship and her circumstances, in order to be able to grasp the internal logic of the text. If structural analysis treats the work as a permutation of universal semantic structures, biographical analysis takes it as evidence of experience, abstracting from the elaboration that makes it a signifying structure for which any personal element is no more than raw material.

It is the unity of a singular point of view, a specific material and a nonetheless universally intelligible symbolic structure that constitutes artistic coherence, unlike, for example, the theoretical coherence that presupposes a language largely stripped of idiosyncratic elements. It is this unity, consequently, that constitutes the difference between cognitive and aesthetic logics. It is in virtue of its unity that a work of art, which is furthermore most often composed of several symbols, is also *one* symbol. Its power is integrally bound up with the elaboration of its 'point of view' and of its own medium, specific language and materials, while the theorist's 'point of view' is not a value in itself but is by definition open to criticism in the name of the coherence of theory—a collective and ongoing work— the medium being that, shared by all, of everyday language and logical and mathematical formalization.

When it succeeds in establishing a novel coherence, the semiotic and semantic innovation introduced by a work of modern art can make a 'language of one' into a 'language for all'. It socializes a hitherto inexpressible experience for which a symbolic formulation did not yet exist. Through artistic work, what had seemed idiosyncratic becomes an exemplary mode of perception and self-expression, a condition accessible to all.

In this respect, art is the only case that escapes the Wittgensteinian verdict on 'private language'. Invented by and for one person, its rules untransposable, its language is at the same time intelligible by all—and if not, it is not art. The symptom is also a 'private language', but it is only accessible to a specialist analysis that unravels the causal fabric of its genesis. The private language of art, often assimilated to madness at its first public appearance, *can* become an integral part of public language. It is madness only for a standardized expressive language, closed to the symbolization of experiences still considered deviant.

The artistic symbol is neither an a priori form to be discovered by the anamnesis of the artist, nor a slip revealing that which escapes conscious language. It is the selection, elaboration and presentation of an unprecedented experience, not yet articulated. Otherwise, it would be impossible to distinguish between a work of art and the skilful imitative reproduction of archetypes, just as one would likewise confuse the slip, the causal and uncontrolled symptom with the artistic symbol that freely constitutes a coherence.

Just like the artistic symbol, the symptom escapes intention. But once deciphered, the symptom generally loses its charm and its mystery together with its ambivalence. The symbol, on the other hand, so far as it is not situated at a level of lucidity lower than that of its interpreter, retains its wealth of significations and possible readings even after analysis. Just as the meaning and truth of a sentence are independent of the intention of the speaker, the symbol escapes intention, not 'beneath' it like the symptom, as a consequence of a causality or unconscious motivation, but 'above' it, in consequence of its auto-explanatory structure. Symbolic coherence has its own life, independent of the meaning it has for its creator.

The symptom calls for a 'deconstructive' interpretation or a 'critique of ideology', the symbol for a 'reconstructive' interpretation or a reading that does justice to its ambition and its success. The 'success' of a symptom is the expression of an intention that can only remain hidden; that of the symbol is the voluntary formal articulation of a constructed meaning. The interpretation of the symptom reveals involuntarily what it signifies 'in truth' and the nature of the illusory intention by virtue of which it does not achieve the status of symbol. The interpretation of the artistic symbol, however, draws on the semantic resources of the work without ever being capable of exhausting them. While being inaccessible to the consciousness of the one who produces it, and despite its ambiguity, the symptom is thus more unequivocal than the symbol. As soon as a symptom is comprehended as such by its involuntary author, it cannot afterwards be reproduced; its causality interrupted and replaced by the use of symbols voluntarily, deliberately generated as such. But between this and the production of artistic symbols, another step remains to be taken. The symptom is a sign of something other than itself, whether it be a sublime reality or a pathological suffering that finds no other means of expression. The artistic symbol, on the other hand, is the sign of nothing but what it makes present; in other words, nothing speaks 'through' it. It has, in principle, no indirect message to deliver—at any rate not as a work of art, though it can evidently be put to secondary uses as historical, sociological or psychological evidence, for example. But as a work, everything it has to say it says or shows itself, without it being necessary to search for a hidden cause behind its signs.

confusions

Much of the criticism and aesthetics of the twentieth century confuses these two readings of art, a confusion explained by certain particularities of modern art. Ideology-critique, psychoanalytic readings and deconstructive interpretation most often treat the symbols of art as the symptoms of unavowable interests or desires. Benjamin treats the architecture of the Paris arcades or the poetry of Baudelaire as clues to the phenomenon of reification, the cult of the new being associated there, as in the fetishism of the commodity, with the eternal return of the same. Adorno makes art the seismograph of a dialectic of Reason. For Derrida, the structure of art makes manifest the self-referential and unfathomable character of all signs, the endless play that characterizes it overwhelming its symbolic autonomy, the work dissolving in the general characteristics of signs and traces. These approaches are characterized by a perpetual ambivalence: as a symptom, the work, deficient and ignorant of what is actually at issue in it, awaits philosophical decipherment; as symbol, it holds the truth about the symptomatic state, on the pathological condition of the world in general, a truth superior to that which philosophy can attain by itself. Art is thus both inferior and superior to philosophy.

In Benjamin, symbol and symptom are inextricably confused in the analysis of the architecture of the arcades, but only the technology that serves as support is truly autonomous. As an engineering construction introducing glass and iron as materials, this architecture tends to free itself from the mythic character of art, its status as a pathological symptom associated with a regressive nostalgia; but by the same token the technology also tends to make art obsolete.[43] For Benjamin, the artistic symbol is identified with a utopia that never succeeds in liberating itself from ideology, so much so that it is indissociably a symptom of false consciousness. It is a 'wish-image' whereby men endeavour to 'overcome and to transfigure' social reality as it exists, 'and the inadequacies of the social organization of production'.[44] As an expression of unsatisfied desires and as the affir-

---

43 Walter Benjamin, 'Paris Capital of the 19th Century', in *Selected Works, 1935–1938*, VOL. 3, trans. Howard Eiland (Cambridge, MA: Belknap/Harvard University Press, 2002), p. 43: 'In the nineteenth century this development worked to emancipate the forms of construction from art, just as in the sixteenth century the sciences freed themselves from philosophy.'

44 Ibid., p. 33.

mation of values whose meaning escapes the subject, art is thus both symptom and symbol. In the same way, in his 'theological' writings Benjamin treats works of art as allegories of a transcendent meaning proper to history as a messianic process.

Writing of the arcades, Benjamin emphasizes only the distinctiveness of the artistic symbol—the fact that it is neither arbitrary game nor lucid knowledge—but he does not grasp its status independent of its ideological or utopian functions. He does not ask how it is that a work 'signifies' and what claims it makes through its mode of symbolization. This is the common failing of all symptomatic approaches to art.

The symptom may be psychological or sociological, depending on whether the unconscious motive is individual or collective, fantasy or ideology. The symbol for its part is irreducible to such a subjective structure. Individually or collectively, the symptom is by definition a pathological phenomenon. For Freud, 'every psychoanalytic treatment is an attempt at liberating repressed love which has found a meagre outlet in the compromise of a symptom',[45] a compromise between an infantile impulse and the normative order of a superego that prohibits its satisfaction. Such a compromise is formed unbeknownst to the subject who cannot accept the desire that inhabits him:

> Symptom formation is a substitute for a symbol whose function has been altered. The split-off symbol has not simply lost all connection with public language. But this grammatical connection has as it were gone underground. It derives its force from confusing the logic of the public usage of language by means of

---

45 Sigmund Freud, 'Jensen's "Gradiva" ', in James Strachey (ed.), *The Standard Edition of the Complete Psychological Works of Sigmund Freud*, VOL. 9 (London: The Hogarth Press and the Institute of Psychoanalysis, 1959).

systematically false identifications. At the level of the public text, the suppressed symbol is objectively understandable through rules resulting from contingent circumstances of the individual's life history, but not connected with it according to intersubjectively recognized rules.[46]

Such an analysis of symptom formation in terms of the theory of language is not to be found as such in Freud, but it is more coherent than a conception that assumes the existence of pre-symbolic representations. Freud himself refused to assimilate the work of art to symptom formation. It has neither the aspect of a causality acting inwardly on freedom of action, nor the character of a compromise between an inadmissible, unacceptable desire and a conventional symbol put to unconventional use. In one way or another, every work of art is an act of freedom that expects to be recognized as such; not indirect evidence, even if a number of artefacts presented as art do not achieve this degree of freedom. According to Freud, the work of art even exhibits certain similarities with the work of the analyst:

> We probably draw from the same source and work upon the same object, each of us by another method. And the agreement of our results seems to guarantee that we have both worked correctly. Our procedure consists in the conscious observation of abnormal mental processes in other people so as to be able to elicit and announce their laws. The author no doubt proceeds differently. He directs his attention to the unconscious of his own mind, he listens to its possible developments and lends them artistic expression instead of suppressing them by conscious criticism. Thus he experiences from himself what we learn from others—the laws which the activities of the uncon-

---

46 Jürgen Habermas, *Knowledge and Human Interests*, trans. Jeremy J. Shapiro (London: Heinemann, 1972), p. 257.

scious must obey. But he need not state these laws, or even be clearly aware of them; as a result of the tolerance of his intelligence, they are incorporated within his creations.[47]

These remarks have been interpreted in two different ways. Some, like Anton Ehrenzweig, see in them a reading of art as an inexhaustible reservoir of unconscious fantasies:

> Freud was pleased to find that he could transfer without much ado the entire inventory of dream interpretation to a new depth-psychological understanding of art. Myths, tragedies, novels, paintings, all carried an undercurrent of symbolic matter. This phantasy content of art could be extracted without difficulty by decoding it according to the catalogue of symbols derived from the interpretation of dreams. Freud found that artists more than others had an instinctive understanding of the unconscious . . . In art the exigencies of unconscious phantasy are often allowed to override the demands of reason and logic. Unconscious phantasy can express itself with less disguise in art than in any other human product, including even jokes.[48]

Here the actual work of the artist is reduced to a non-professional attention to the unconscious in which the real expert is the psychoanalyst. As for the 'catalogue of symbols' discovered in art—a formulation that recalls Jung—this is in reality the entirety of the symptoms decoded by the interpretation of dreams which it 'rediscovers' in art without strictly having any need of this illustrative detour. Art here has only a documentary value, offering nothing that psychoanalysis has not learnt by its own means.

---

47 Freud, 'Gradiva', p. 92.

48 Anton Ehrenzweig, *The Hidden Order of Art* (London: Weidenfeld & Nicholson, 1967), pp. 266–7.

The other reading of Freud attributes to the artist a process of constructive reflection that presents not fantasy in the 'naked' state but always a symbolic articulation capable, in its own logic and its own 'language', of rivalling any analyst in critical insight. Gilles Deleuze thus distinguishes—in vitalist but non-reductive terms—between literature and the production of pathological symptoms:

> We do not write with our neuroses. Neuroses or psychoses are not passages of life, but states into which we fall when the process is interrupted, blocked, or plugged up . . . Moreover, the writer as such is not a patient but rather a physician, the physician of himself and of the world. The world is the set of symptoms whose illness merges with man. Literature then appears as an enterprise of health.[49]

On the other hand, 'when the delirium falls back into the *clinical state*, words no longer open out onto anything, we no longer hear or see anything through them but a night whose history, colours and song have been lost. Literature is a health',[50] more precisely an 'irresistible and delicate health',[51] which means, notwithstanding the medical terminology, that art does not call for symptomatic interpretation.

What encourages the confusion between symptom and symbol in relation to works of art is the fact that artistic creation is an activity in which the subject is passionately involved. The detachment of the virtuoso artist, maintaining a radical separation between his personal life and his handling of artistic techniques, is only one aspect of this process, that which has to do with the autonomy of the symbol. But what fascinates in a work of

---

49 Gilles Deleuze, 'Literature and Life' in *Essays Critical and Clinical*, trans. Daniel W. Smith and Michael A. Greco (London: Verso, 1998), p. 3.

50 Ibid., p. lv.

51 Ibid., p. 3.

103

art is that this coolness conceals an experience and a vulnerability without which the work of art would be no more than a *combinatoire*. The artistic symbol is distinguishable from the arbitrarily reproducible artefact by the fact that it masters a limit experience by giving it form—arising, as it were, on the ruins of a symptom.

A critic's analysis can insist either on the sometimes pathological experience that underlies a work—thus leaving aside what makes it art— or on the constructive labour that symbolizes detachment from and reflection on the experience. This is aptly illustrated in an essay of Donald Kuspit's on Baselitz. The editorial introduction that precedes the text promises a 'psychoanalytic reading' that discovers in these paintings 'the sovereignty of the archaic, narcissistic ego. An immature, unsocialized ego, all of whose contradictions are manifested in his inverted figures.'[52] One thus expects an essay that deciphers and unmasks pathological symptoms, but in fact Kuspit's argument is much more subtle. Rather than adopting the attitude of the psychoanalyst, he credits the artist with a reflection on the pathology that he exhibits, seeing in his painting not the simple production of symptoms but an authentically artistic labour of symbolization. Otherwise he would not begin his article by saying that 'Baselitz is one of the great contemporary painters, to whom we owe the restoration of the credibility of painting, and of figurative painting in particular.'[53]

Kuspit is struck by the contrast, in Baselitz, between 'a lack of maturity' in the figure and the 'plenitude of the painting'.[54]

> Baselitz reveals the archaic, narcissistic self that underlies abstraction and is dissimulated in it. One might think of

---

52 Donald Kuspit, 'Le moi archaïque de Georg Baselitz', *Art Press* 77 (January 1984), p. 4.

53 Ibid., p. 5.

54 Ibid.

abstract art, in fact, as no more than aesthetic narcissism mistakenly understood as autonomy. Abstraction represents a withdrawal from reality and a retreat to the only notion of the self it still allows, if only behind the ironic mask of style. Baselitz's figure signals that the archaic self is ridding itself of its abstract garb as if it no longer found it necessary, given that the real itself seems to have become abstract . . . Baselitz does not reinvent the figure: he unveils the narcissistic self that today has become post-historic, having failed to change history, to revolutionize the world.[55]

What seems to embody the regressive aspects of Neo-Expressionism is thus seen as a reflection on the fate of abstract painting, on its false emancipation and its reductive politicization. According to Kandinsky's account, abstraction came to him on his seeing a painting of his own upside-down, and it is this inversion that Baselitz perpetually reproduces as he exploits the tension between the expansion of pictorial autonomy thus engendered and the figurative origin that is never entirely escaped and which retains its own power of evocation. The primitive, inverted figure, pulled upward by the powerful draw of gravity, symbolizes painting's invincible resistance to a surface intellectualism. For Kuspit:

Baselitz's importance lies in his restoring to us a sense of the archaism that is the true foundation of modern art, and his suggesting that his primitivism is the instrument by which he preserves the existence of the self against all comers. The experience of modernity has taught us to distrust those who offer us a unitary 'ready-made' self, what Baselitz calls 'the new-style self'. Baselitz's figures, contorted in their archaic grandiosity, offer a conflicted alternative to the high-performance, functional style of the self. This entirely socialized self has an illusory sense of

---

55 Ibid.

its own grandeur, convinced as it is of the sense of mastery afforded to it by a mechanical, robotic society. Baselitz's figures reject this compliant and conformist self, regressing to an archaic self too narcissistic to find its place in the system.[56]

The privileging of Baselitz is admittedly debatable, but hardly any more so than a commitment to an art as 'mode of social expression both sophisticated and ironic, in which irony barely succeeds in avoiding conformism'.[57] And very likely Kuspit fails to appreciate the diversity of the works that he lumps together under 'abstraction'. To a struggle around a definition of an art worthy of the name that had become sterile and dogmatic in the debates around Post-Minimalism and Conceptualism, he opposes an endeavour that he finds highly instructive. In art, there is no risk-free option because there is no art without partisanship. Baselitz's deliberate 'regression', the source of his 'powerful painterliness' *can* be interpreted as the expression of collective fantasies and attitudes that the artist contents himself with transcribing. Kuspit himself makes several references to the German context of Baselitz's painting, but without claiming that the painter's 'Neo-Expressionism' is reducible to a regressive collective mentality and as such purely symptomatic. He shows that the artist produces his symbols in reflecting on both painterly tradition and history. Even if Kuspit is wrong about the lucidity of the painter, whose nationalistic observations he underplays, he offers an example of a criticism that interprets and evaluates a difficult body of work as art, rather than as a symptomatic document.

An idealism of the symbolic sees artistic creation as a sublime endeavour perfectly transparent to itself; a symptom-decoding anti-idealism is based on a disenchanted sympathy with the imperfect, fallible creature, delivered up to sin; so it is that the distinctive semiologies of 'Catholics'

---

56 Ibid., p. 7.

57 Ibid.

and 'Protestants' reflect two opposed conceptions of human nature. If the Kantianism of Cassirer or the iconology of Panofsky suggests the creation and unmuddied transmission of autonomous symbolic forms, the deconstructive history of art cultivates the ambiguity of opaque symptoms, inexhaustible in the face of interpretation, an ambiguity that undermines the proud and illusory autonomy of reason.

In *Confronting Images*, Georges Didi-Huberman expounds an aesthetic of the symptom conceived as a critique of an idealist history of art; he thus offers a remarkable example of the deconstruction of the concept of the aesthetic symbol in the name of the concept of symptom. This concept has two different aspects. Firstly, it refers to a distinction (between *studium* and *punctum*) that Barthes introduced into the discussion of photography, between studious contemplation and captivation by incongruous detail. For Barthes, the *punctum* is the uncontrollable experience of the photograph as it transmits the shock of the real.[58] This experience is not 'aesthetic' in the sense of grasping the structure and the constitutive ambition of a work; the *punctum* is not necessarily the same for every viewer. Barthes is struck by a boy's 'bad teeth',[59] yet there is nothing to stop someone else from noticing his shirt or the braces of the child on the left of the picture, etc.

Secondly, the symptom is—this time in painting—the sign of the work of the unconscious. It is no longer a question of true chance but of a construction that escapes its author. As Didi-Huberman says: 'The symptom causes to pass before our eyes the event of an encounter in which the *constructed share* of the work staggers under the shock and violation of a *cursed share* that is central to it.'[60] This is how he describes Dürer's *Man of Sorrows*:

---

58 Roland Barthes, *Camera Lucida*, trans. Richard Howard (London: Vintage, 1993).

59 Ibid., p. 45.

60 Didi-Huberman, *Confronting Images*, pp. 115–16.

> We are here besieged [*investis*] by the dimension of the symptom, to the very extent that the body of Christ withdraws into itself *before* us as in a kind of refusal to remain visible. It's like looking intently at a contracting fist: a hand has closed, convulsively, and because it closes it delivers nothing but the symptom of its withdrawal, whose secret will remain concealed in the hollow of the palm . . . Symptom of a flesh delivered up to the unhappy autoscopia of its own wounds.[61]

In fact, this description relates not to a symptomatic work but to one perfectly 'symbolic', and is in fact a 'content analysis' of a work showing a man rigid with pain. But what there is here is not an artistic 'symptom' but the symbolic representation of—if you like—'symptoms' of pain and suffering. A description that, without preconceived ideas, attended to the phenomenon of the work itself, drawing attention, if need be, to aspects neglected by other interpreters, would not find an aesthetic symptom. Nothing here in fact escapes the stylizing intention of the artist, and its seems to me that the concept of symptom is here robbed of its significance.

'Panofsky's attempt, like Cassirer's,' Didi-Huberman says elsewhere, 'pertained then to what might be called "pre-Freudian" reason.'[62] The Freudian approach, on the other hand, 'focused on the symptom as something that breaks up all discursive unity, as what intrudes upon and smashes the whole order of the Idea, opens systems and imposes something unthinkable'.[63] But the operation of art—as was stressed by Freud himself, as we have seen—is not analogous to the involuntary and uncontrollable advent of the symptom. Art is not this other of 'discursive unity' constituted by the symptom when it 'signifies' by a slip of the tongue or a failure to

---

61 Ibid., pp. 175–7.

62 Ibid., p. 170.

63 Ibid., p. 169.

act, without attaining to the status of a constructed symbol, adopted and presented as such. The work of art's rupture with perceptual and intellectual stereotypes has nothing to do with the disorder of the spontaneous unconscious. It addresses itself to the intelligence, not in order to be delivered of a stifled compulsion but in order to be taken seriously, understood and recognized in terms of its self-articulated aesthetic ambitions. The real otherness of the work of art seems to me to reside in its aesthetic ambition, which, today, is most often accessible only to a patient experience of the work rather than through its apparent references to facts made familiar and suggestive to us by recent history.

interferences

Yet this relationship between symbol and symptom in the work of art can never be reduced to indifference. The artistic symbol is not a grammatical example; it is itself the fruit of a *quest* for symbolization. The artistic symbol is not radically disassociated from the symptomatic order, because what is at issue in art is neither the logical nor the grammatical. Its signs refer to experiences that are to be shared and which are never merely instructive. In the artistic symbol, unlike the linguistic or logico-mathematical symbol, the signifier cannot be employed *ad libitum* and by anybody. Philosophies of language that refuse to admit the conventional character of the sign take precisely the artistic symbol as their model, generalizing from it impermissibly.[64]

---

[64] Walter Benjamin, 'On Language as Such and on the Language of Man', in *Selected Writings, 1913–1926*, VOL. 1, p. 69: 'The human word is the name of things. Hence it is no longer conceivable, as the bourgeois view of language maintains, that the word has an accidental relation to its object, that it is a sign for things (or knowledge of them) agreed by some convention.'

In the modern period, which more than any earlier age creates the conditions for the social and psychological isolation of the individual and the destabilization of identity, the work of art is a symbol won by great struggle from an experience frequently symptomatic or pathological. All the more reason, then, not to confound it with that experience, as if it were content to testify to it. The artistic symbol confers on its symptomatic origins a general intelligibility, 'idealizing' in its stylization, and demands of the beholder a symmetrical idealization without which the work cannot be taken seriously as such but only examined as a symptom of the subject who presents it. When the beholder believes himself capable of acceding directly to the experience that he discovers, he forgets the artificial—constructed and reflective—nature of the symbol that evokes the experience, by which the singularity of individual lived experience is transformed into a 'language for all'. When it succeeds, artistic work makes a symbol of an experience that has not yet found a language but which aspires to escape the isolation of the idiosyncratic in order to be shared.

It would certainly be wrong to subsume under this model the whole of the traditional art of the past, most often based on collective experiences articulated before the creation of the work and a stranger to the modern taste for radical innovation. But one could equally defend the position that modern, anti-traditionalist art is the only art that fully satisfies aesthetic criteria, being irreducible to visions of the world to be found in philosophy or other disciplines (religious, theoretical, moral, artisanal, etc.). For a work of art that does no more than illustrate a concept given by a representation of the imagination[65] does not meet the criteria of specificity that distinguishes the artistic schema from other types of coherence.

---

65 'In a word, an aesthetic idea is a presentation of the imagination which is conjoined with a given concept' (Kant, *Critique of Judgment*, ss. 49, p. 185).

The concept of novelty should not be confused with the function that it fulfils in certain philosophies of history that give it the status of a completely other [*tout-autre*], centering on it the hope of deliverance or reconciliation. Such is the messianic status of the art of the future from the Romantics to the radical avant-gardes of the twentieth century and their philosophical spokesmen. During this period of almost two centuries, the expectation of large-scale historical change has regularly turned to the prophetic signs represented by innovative art in which one thought to glimpse an index of the completely other. Here there is no question of artistic interest as such but of a promise inherent in the work that goes beyond it. It is true that the possibility of a radically new perspective in the realm of art is not independent of the profane history that makes it possible—no work of power is invented in abstraction—but it is wrong to try and deduce concrete historic solutions or, even more so, messianic reconciliations, from such as do emerge; at the very most, art may—at the risk of error—anticipate likely problems or developments. What enables an artist to translate his idiosyncratic experience into a formal 'language' capable of being shared is the fact that hidden beneath its idiosyncrasy are exemplary aspects which are as such communicable, provided that the means to evoke them are found.

In the works of pre-modern times, there is not so radical a rupture between artistic generations but changes of style that preserve a fundamental continuity of ideas about the meaning and function of art; nor is there an individuality presenting a radical singularity and so shocking and incomprehensible; examples of such artists have been essentially been 'rediscovered' in the modern age. Prehistory, Antiquity and the Middle Ages offer few 'mad' artists: at the most 'outlaws' whose language remains perfectly intelligible. The oddity of an art based on a 'language for one' is specific to modernity.

In the present age, art has become the receptacle of every kind of deviation from a repressive or intolerant normality. It assumes the role of socializing the excluded and represents the right of individuals to what Adorno called unregulated experience. This being so, it was possible for the multiplication of artistic experiment to become an end in itself, legitimate without reference to the degree of aesthetic quality achieved in any individual case. In modern art, dissonance and negativity have achieved a more fundamental status than in the past, a status that has been interpreted in different ways.[66]

Certainly, to say that Kafka, Schönberg and Beckett present in their works the experiences of a 'decentered subjectivity freed from the constraints of everyday knowledge and activity'[67] is hardly to account for the emphatic ambition of their works, of the exorcism that they effect of a reality lived as absolute negativity. To see in this an effort to transform the subject and to reintegrate the heteroclite, the excluded and the repressed into the communication of all[68] is to instrumentalize an intention at first more critical than constructive. It would perhaps be more correct to say that the aggressively negative presentation of a reality seen as catastrophic refers implicitly to the demand for a depathologized life, a demand without which art as an effort to realize the coherence of experience could

---

66 'the . . . neutralization of the good, the useful, and the true—the aesthetic rebellion against all norms . . . purifies aesthetic experience . . . from admixtures of different value spheres' (Jürgen Habermas, *The New Conservatism: Cultural Criticism and the Historians' Debate*, ed. and trans. Shierry Weber Nicholsen, Cambridge: Polity Press, 1989, p. 29ff.). For Adorno, on the other hand, this negativity expresses above all 'the real negativity of the social situation' (Adorno, *Aesthetic Theory*, p. 21. See also Menke's interpretation in his *Sovereignty of Art*).

67 Habermas, *The New Conservatism*, p. 29.

68 Albrecht Wellmer, 'Truth, Semblance and Reconciliation', *Telos* 62 (1984/85), p. 103.

hardly be conceived of. All incompletion, all dissonant aggression and all disintegration of art make a nod to the traditional expectation of harmony; the disintegrated work always being presented *in place of* the work harmoniously achieved, just as since the Renaissance the artist has always presented the profane reality of the self-portrait or the still life *in place of* the sacred icon. This tendency towards homoeostasis is independent of any religious foundation to art. The aesthetic logic has always already begun to emancipate itself from the sacred; it tends to render superfluous any normative reference to any religion whatsoever, contenting itself with immanent achievement. What gives art the *appearance* of the sacred is the fact that this achievement transcends the world of empirical experience.

Creative art has always been drawn to realities hitherto excluded or unperceived, by the possible not yet realizable except in the imagination and in the sphere of the non-quotidian. Subjectivity in free communication with itself creates a work only to the extent that it occupies an empty place in culture, in other words it responds to an unmet desire. This is why art has a particular affinity with the pathologies of its age; it is also the reason for the connection between the dimensions of expression and evaluation, of the aesthetic and the therapeutic. Meaning that is not yet publicly recognized appears in the guise of a pathological reality, until it is integrated into the common language.[69] Identified with the pathology that he makes manifest, the innovative artist first appears as sick, perverse, deviant, provocative. It is, then, a particular blindspot of the common languages that is targeted by an innovative work of art.

As far back as one goes in the history of modern times, the great movements of artistic innovation have been seen as threatening pathologies before becoming the mainstays of the academicism in whose name

---

[69] See my article 'Langage pour un, langage pour tous', *Critique*, 488–489 (January–February 1988), pp. 95–113.

the succeeding innovation will be condemned. The very names of the movements—Mannerism, Baroque, Rococo—are expressions of the sickly or bizarre; Goethe opposed Romanticism to Classicism as sickness to health; 'realism' is as much an insult as a boast; since Impressionism, the series of -isms and Arts (Fauvism, Cubism, Minimalism, Pop Art, Conceptual Art, Arte Povera, etc.) is composed of nicknames or epithets often coined by unsympathetic critics then adopted or rejected by those responsible for them. What has each time conferred on these movements a kind of necessity, what has brought them recognition and admission into the 'history of art', has been their adequacy to an experience stamped by negativity from which they succeeded in winning a constructive potential by converting impoverishment into expressive wealth, symptom into symbol.

If innovative art is not analysable in terms of symptom, whatever may be the pathological ground it raises to the rank of symbolic experience, mass art, on the other hand, like a popular cinema perfectly achieved in terms of technique, most often does not attempt the aesthetic symbolization of the issues it tackles, remaining a mere vehicle for collective fantasy. This is true more particularly of the disaster-movie, of the myths of Evil or of the sorcerer's apprentice in American culture, from King Kong to the dinosaurs. A conformist culture in this way discharges its violence against the monsters that threaten its imaginary innocence, its rigid identity and need for security. To say that productions that content themselves with the effective embodiment of collective fantasies are not 'art' in the same way as self-reflexive works, and that both are to be evaluated in terms of the pleasure they afford to the individual, is to cheaply sacrifice one of the gains of modern aesthetics: its demand for maturity and accountability. Whatever is said, we make a distinction between a work that holds our intelligence in contempt in feeding us on primitive images of the most widely shared desires and anxieties, and a work that distances these images and their content in ideas in order to present, through critical symbolization, a vision that illuminates us.

Yet this distinction does not at all coincide with the traditional hierarchy between mass art and art of quality;[70] in 'high' art one finds vulgarity, crass ideology, unjustified pretension and concession to the taste of the day, just as in 'mass art' one can find examples of finesse, of unpretentious subtlety, critical thinking and innovation. Given that the traditional divisions are no longer operative, it for our judgement to discover the works that deserve attention and admiration.

---

70 See Wellmer, 'Truth, Semblance and Reconciliation', pp. 112ff., and Richard Shusterman, 'Form and Funk: The Aesthetic Challenge of Popular Art' in *Pragmatic Aesthetics: Living, Beauty, Rethinking Art* (Oxford: Basil Blackwell, 1992), pp. 169–200.

judgements and preferences: aesthetic pragmatics

Deleuze rightly points out that it is in a critique of *judgement* that Kant introduces aesthetics. Yet it is for this same reason that he rejects such an approach himself, following Nietzsche in his suspicion of judgement: 'Kant did not invent a true critique of judgment; on the contrary, what the book of this title established was a fantastic subjective tribunal.'[71] Judgement is seen as a falsely rational way of dealing with the phenomenon of art, a physical, sensual and energetic phenomenon and as such considered as a counterweight to modern reason.

In France, this defence of a reality salvaged from the depredations of reason is associated with a tradition of opposition to power; in Germany, it is exclusive to conservatism. Against Kantian reason, Heidegger and Gadamer attempt, in Marquard's words, 'a resurrection of the self-evidence of what goes without saying, otherwise lost'.[72] Judgement appears here as

---

71 Deleuze, *Essays Critical and Clinical*, p. 126.

72 Odo Marquard, 'Indicted and Unburdened Man in Eighteenth-Century Philosophy' in *Farewell to Matters of Principle*: *Philosophical Studies*, trans. Robert M. Wallace (Oxford: Oxford University Press, 1989), p. 52. [Translation modified.]

playing gooseberry to artistic *jouissance*. But judgement repressed makes an implicit return in the selection of works and the analysis of what is at stake in them, although these operations too are meant to escape the realm of reason, the 'psychology of the priest'. For art seems to be the domain of an empathy in which body, perception, sensation and affect keep their distance from reason to affirm being directly, i.e. without reason's mediation.

Such a neutralization of judgement is no more than illusory. Once identified, the judgement that returns in the choices made can also be the object of critique and rational justification. Just as a personal opinion is not called 'true' (nor a partisan position 'just' or a manifest expression of bad faith 'sincere'), an object that pleases only one person is not called a work of art. The word 'beautiful' is not used of a purely personal pleasure. As if anticipating the theory of linguistic usage, Kant writes:

> It would be ridiculous if someone who prided himself on his taste tried to justify it by saying: This object (the building we are looking at, the garment that man is wearing, the concert we are listening to, the poem put up to be judged) is beautiful *for me*. For he must not call it *beautiful* if [he means] only [that] he likes it . . . . But if he proclaims something to be beautiful, then he requires the same liking from others; he then judges it not just for himself, but for everyone, and speaks of beauty as if it were a property of things.[73]

This observation is of great import, and not only in aesthetics. But not having the conceptual resources to draw out all its implications, Kant was unable to exploit them in their entirety. To grasp the radically open character of the debate on truth, justice and aesthetic value—which cannot be set-

---

73 Kant, *Critique of Judgment*, ss. 7, pp. 55–6.

tled by a reflexive, transcendental approach but requires argument between different points of view—he would have had to be able to anticipate the shift from a philosophy of consciousness in the Cartesian tradition to a philosophy of language, from a philosophy of the transcendental subject to a philosophy of intersubjectivity, from an atemporal philosophy to a thought of reason situated in history. This was a move made possible only by a series of important crises provoked in philosophy by its confrontation with historical experience, the exact sciences and the human and social sciences.

It is possible, without contradiction, to claim that this or that is 'good', 'agreeable' or 'interesting' only for me (or for us, the members of a group or even a community). On the other hand, to say that a thing cannot—without a contradiction in terms—be 'true', 'just', 'sincere' or 'beautiful' (or 'a successful work of art') *only for me,* is to say that these notions engage the interests of all, in other words, the entire diversity of points of view that can exist in a society. It also means, at the same time, that I undertake, when I express myself, to offer more than a subjective opinion, that I believe I have reasons that will allow me to respond to any contestation; that my point of view can be refuted by other arguments, and in consequence revised, to the extent that I am led to accept such convincing criticism. If I claim then, as a subject, a more than subjective relevance for my assessment, it is because I have reason to believe that it is defensible so far. But I also know that it may have to admit other argued points of view that take account of aspects I have neglected, interests or considerations that I have been unaware of or ignored, evaluations that I could not anticipate. I am thus prepared to enter an open-ended discussion intended to establish the status of commitments that are each time put into question.

Everyday life is structured by such commitments to universality, though this is hidden by the fact that they do not appear as such except in the case of explicit problematization or thematization. It is only in the case of contestation that it is necessary to justify ones judgement or actions by having recourse to developed argument. This is equally true in the field of art. What escapes a positivist or empiricist approach to aesthetic judgement is this idea of *sharing* that is inherent in the use of the adjective 'beautiful' when applied to a successful work, i.e. in aesthetic 'pragmatics'. Once we experience an artistic pleasure, in the sense that we think that a work is so accomplished or successful that all should see it as we do, we are going beyond the realm of private sensations. What it seems needs to be preserved of the Kantian Idea is the notion of a *normative bond* between persons, established by virtue of the fact that they see the reasons for which a work justifiably claims to be successful and artistically significant. This involves an intersubjective necessity designated by the adjective 'beautiful' properly when employed as an aesthetic judgement.

Kant confuses the aesthetic reasons capable of grounding a judgement of beauty with the determination of the object of knowledge by the scientific concept. This is why he falls into the dilemma of a 'subjective necessity' that allows anyone, against all reason, to maintain his personal judgement of taste.[74] At the same time, he holds up in the 'aesthetic Idea' the vision, far beyond this bond, of a relationship with the 'supersensible' or the absolute, that our reason cannot attain to. This is why both Positivists and Romantics have been able to lay claim to Kant.

Like other forms of knowledge, aesthetics is open to argument, even though rigorous 'proof' has no place in it. If it is not possible for me bring another to *love* a work (any more than to love a person), I can at least adduce reasons in support of my belief that it is successful or not, If it is

---

[74] 'I shall stop my ears, shall refuse to listen to reasons or arguments, and shall sooner assume that those rules of the critics are at fault, or at least do not apply to the present case, than allow my judgment to be determined by a priori bases of proof. For it is meant to be a judgment of taste, and not one of the understanding or reason' (ibid., ss. 33, p. 148).

contradictory to say that 'this is beautiful—for me,' this means that it is possible to justify ones judgement; the 'aesthetic rationality' that specifies the modalities of such justification, which Kant for systematic reasons was able merely to glimpse, escapes both positivist reductionism and the excesses of speculative aesthetics.

aesthetic judgement and idiosyncratic judgement

Love of a person or object or a personal preference for a work or an art are not susceptible to argument. The same is true of most forms of pleasure. Not all pleasures are sensual and, in that sense, aesthetic; the pleasure or joy that we experience on hearing good news for ourselves or for another, on receiving a gift or a kindness or on hearing a witticism or a rapier-like riposte, are moral or intellectual satisfactions. Aesthetic pleasure is related to the pleasurable perception of sounds, forms, colours or combinations thereof, such as are found in nature or in the cultural world. The fact that there is in this as yet nothing of the specifically aesthetic becomes clear as soon as we think of its contrary, displeasure, and the judgements that we make on objects that displease us. What is aesthetically disagreeable, ugly, gross, clumsy or repugnant, provokes our disapproval whether in objects or in real scenes, but this disapproval answers to no expectation on the part of the objects in question. On the other hand, the artistic representation of a displeasing object, like the presentation of an abstract work in colours or forms conventionally considered 'ugly', can be 'artistically beautiful' or worthy of interest. If we judge it to be ugly, it is in a sense different from the first case. For the 'ugliness' of a work of art has to do not with what it refers to, nor simply the aesthetic means that it employs, but with its 'spirit' as manifested in its formal choices. Sensual and sensuous as it may be, the pleasure afforded us by a work of art is never separable from its 'spirit'. This becomes clear in the comparison of a commonplace, vulgar photograph of a beautiful body and a beautiful photograph of a body lacking in canonical proportions but transfigured by love or intelligence. Even in its sensuality, artistic pleasure is subject to symbolic criteria.[75] A cultural product that lays claim to the title of art and which offers *no* pleasure of this intellectual or affective kind generally remains on the threshold of the world of art and does not enter its realm.[76]

I can admire the literary (stylistic[77]) qualities of a scientific text, the strange beauty of an aeroplane or the rhythm of a train in motion. The potential to make aesthetic experience of realities of every kind—whose primary ambition is not aesthetic and which can exist or fulfil their functions even in the absence of these secondary qualities—is without limit. Yet it has no 'normative' implication. A scientific text without any aesthetic qualities might be perfectly valid *qua* scientific text.

A work of art can be considered to be such even if the feelings it evokes are hardly formulable in terms of pleasure. Modern works such as *Guernica* or an abstract by Barnett Newman inspire fear or unease rather than 'pleasure' in the primary sense of the term, and the experience of listening to certain modern musical works can suggest a session of torture skilfully distilled by the composer, without the attentive eye or ear being tempted to turn away. One can say then that in one way or another they

---

75 Adorno, *Aesthetic Theory*, p. 87: 'The sensual exists in art only spiritualized and refracted.'

76 Danto makes a subtle distinction between a simple object 'excluded' from art exhibitions, and Duchamp's urinal, 'rejected' by the hanging committee of the Salon des Indépendants (*The Philosophical Disenfranchisement of Art*, p. 32). One could equally well say that a work rejected as such, for good reasons, is assimilated to the nature of a mere fabricated object, whose claim to the dignity of art is refused. But this would imply a judgement of value that Danto precisely wishes to avoid.

77 See Genette, *Fiction and Diction*, p. 28.

find a certain 'pleasure' or 'satisfaction', in the sense in which Kant, speaking of the sublime, spoke of a pleasure preceded by unpleasure. The register of pleasure/unpleasure is no doubt always present in aesthetic experience. How though can it be defined—in comparison with culinary or sexual pleasure, the perverse pleasure of the voyeur, the pleasure of flying over water or snow—if not in terms of shared necessities or 'reasons' related both to the structure of the work, its claim to recognition or its significance, and to the fact, as Kant nonetheless puts it, that it can 'supply a wealth of undeveloped material to the understanding'?[78]

Description as a 'work of art' necessarily involves a normative dimension not implied in describing a text as 'literary'.[79] Good or bad, a text may display the characteristics of a literary text; it could, for example, respect the relatively strict rules of the sonnet or the much more flexible rules of the novel. Nevertheless, when the lines are so far-fetched that no intelligible meaning can be detected in what claims to be a poem, or when cliché is piled upon cliché and the images are utterly lacking in originality, why does one hesitate to speak of a 'work of art'? Is it simply a question of prejudice or intolerance? Or are their technical or normative limits to the recognition of an artefact as a work of art? It is clear that these limits cannot be defined once and for all. They are established on the basis of criteria whose content changes and develops with the history of the arts and

---

78 Kant, *Critique of Judgement,* ss. 49, p. 185.

79 See Adorno, *Aesthetic Theory,* pp. 164–5: 'The question, however, of what is and what is not a work of art cannot in any way be separated from the faculty of judging, that is, from the question of quality, of good and bad. The idea of a bad artwork has something nonsensical about it: If it miscarries, if it fails to achieve its immanent constitution, it fails its own concept and sinks beneath the a priori of art.' There remains the question of the criteria by which one judges a work good or bad; Adorno's mistake is to think that the 'dialectic of reason' is sufficient to answer the question.

the history of judgement, and cannot therefore be defined in an abstract, procedural manner.

There does not exist a *type of discourse* that can be identified a priori as belonging to the genre of the 'literary work of art', as there does exist a type of discourse that is 'scientific' (leaving aside the fact that this type of discourse does not in itself guarantee that a discourse that adopts its characteristics will in fact be accepted as a contribution to science). In the same way, there does not exist a type of graphic expression, of application of paint or production of objects that may be unambiguously ascribed to art. Every publisher receives manuscripts that resemble works of art—which are indeed neither scientific texts, nor simple heaps of paper claiming to be both literary works and works of art—but which, though they may often manifest a 'literary tone', are not necessarily works of art. In the same way, galleries often receive submissions that prove unacceptable. The description 'work of art' does not depend simply on the semantic and pragmatic conditions of a genre of discourse. It is legitimately applied only if it is based on a competent judgement that involves an assessment of relevance or 'success' and originality.[80]

Efforts to delimit art from non-art focused first of all on the literary, for the simple reason that language is, more than any other, the artistic medium used mostly for non-artistic purposes. But increasingly, with the development of a culture of reproduction and the inflationary proliferation of the image, this problem has been posed in the visual arts. The endeavours of Duchamp and Warhol reflect the necessity, in this domain, of responding to the challenge represented by industrial production and reproduction.

---

80 In both cases, the discovery that an artefact is the work of a counterfeiter or copyist is a bar to its recognition as a work of art. The concept of the latter allows for certain forms of appropriation or carelessness of originality so long as these reflect a new and relevant signifying intention.

The fact that there can be no a priori definition of what a work of art must be does not justify the elimination of all criteria of evaluation in the definition of art. Danto, who defends the work of art's independence from appreciation, nonetheless admits that 'we cannot characterize works of art without in the same breath evaluating them.'[81] If the fact of its being positively evaluated or otherwise implies little for its status as a work of art,[82] it is not in fact insignificant that no more in aesthetics than in ethics is it possible to radically dissociate description from evaluation (positive or negative). One cannot understand a work of art or an action affecting the interests of other persons without taking account of the conditions in which this work or this action are acceptable as such. It is not a matter of privileging, in the name of some norm established a priori, those works of art judged 'good'; it is not a question either of finding a work good or bad under arbitrarily generalized criteria. It is a matter of taking account of the fact that the evaluative dimension cannot be excluded from descriptive analysis if this claims to grasp its object in terms of the claim that is intrinsic to it: an object that lays claim to the status of art is not just 'there', like a stone or a table. It is this that gives its 'normative' character to every relationship to a work of art. To attempt to follow or survey a work of art, to describe it as a work, one has to anticipate a structure and meaning by virtue of a certain normative expectation of achievement and success. It is obviously possible to describe it from a non-aesthetic point of view, as a linguistic or narrative text, as an image or an object, as a fabric of sounds or noises, while bracketing off the question of aesthetic validity. One could describe a work of Tinguely's as one might describe a crane, a tractor or

---

81 Danto, *The Transfiguration of the Commonplace*, p. 156.

82 Ibid., p. 92: 'To restrict to the favorable cases the application of the epithet "work of art" would be parallel to regarding moral considerations as arising only with persons and actions which had some "minimal potential value or worthiness".'

a pump, providing the maximum of technical detail, without bringing in the slightest notion of art; but one would not then be describing it *as a work of art*. A specialist in poetics could construct a tale deploying the maximum number of narrative modes and techniques, and these would then be describable without the least aesthetic appreciation. This would be a 'grammatical' exercise that claimed to offer neither meaning nor aesthetic satisfaction but that might nonetheless afford pleasures and unpleasures of many kinds. In the case of a work of art, a description of this kind, aesthetically speaking, manifests an objectivizing attitude that is alien to the attitude of aesthetic perception. The same goes, more or less, for an act that affects more than one person: if one wants to understand its morality, it is equally impossible to abstain from any appreciation of its acceptability and so the adoption of a normative stance. In describing a social phenomenon, such as an action or a work of art, it is impossible to abstract from any and every commitment because any description implies choices and value-judgements.

The criteria by which an artefact may or may not be described as art are integral elements of a critical 'procedure', a process of argumentation, but such criteria may nonetheless be delimited. Leaving behind the excessive rigour characteristic of dogmatic approaches—of which the ideologies of the avant-gardes were the latest embodiment—aesthetic theory has now fallen into the opposite trap, with the expression of preferences purely personal or specific to sectarian schools, a 'blue-chip' conformism, a sardonic and provocative non-conformism displayed in the taste for certain culture-industry phenomena, an almost limitless tolerance, and, in the last analysis, a certain embarrassed indifference towards art.

Kant distinguishes aesthetic judgement from both theoretical and moral judgement and from estimations of the useful and the agreeable. In doing this he argues from the way in which we use the word 'beautiful'. We call 'beautiful' that which pleases independently of all moral or cognitive interest, of all notions of utility or personal inclination.[83] Once one considers this use of language independently of the presuppositions of the Kantian system, it evokes a normative demand that does not at all prejudge our relationships to nature but governs the relations of reciprocal expectation and demand established between a work of art and its audience. It is the *rule* of a language game. To say that something is beautiful, when speaking of something that simply suits our own private, idiosyncratic taste, is, in Wittgensteinian terms, to say that you are hurting while you are in no pain or to say that you see something red when seeing something blue: it is to be mistaken about an established practice, grounded in a basic consensus transmitted by socialization. But such usage is not simply transmitted de facto, but governed by a logic that is not purely conventional. It is this aesthetic logic that gives the rule its normative character.

According to Kant, the universality of the beautiful is 'subjective', but in a sense that engages every subject; it is only in the fictive mode of the 'as if' that it refers to an objective quality of the object: one then 'speaks of beauty as if it were a property of things'.[84] In reality, it involves only a certain relation between our subjective faculties, an accord between the cognitive faculties addressed by the object. For Kant, the beautiful object appeals to 'the indeterminate idea of the supersensible in us',[85] an idea common to all that testifies to the agreement between our mind and the sensible world. This is why it is impossible, according to Kant, to adduce proofs in support of an aesthetic judgement,[86] for this would be to determine the object in conceptual terms according to the principle of determinant judgement.

---

83 Kant, *Critique of Judgement,* ss. 6 and 7.

84 Ibid., ss. 7, p. 56.

85 Ibid., ss. 57, pp. 213–14.

Although he refers to language use, Kant thus continues to identify this with a purely denotative determination, so much so that in the case of aesthetic judgement this can only involve a pseudo-determination of the object and not a positive evaluation based on objective qualities. Kant is obliged to treat language as a matter of subjective faculties because he cannot conceive of different modes of object-reference. Aesthetic judgement determines the qualities of the object not in order to know them (in the manner of scientific knowledge), but to grasp the formal organization of the symbols that evoke the coherence and suggestive wealth of an actualizable vision. In the absence of real reference, there is nothing to denote; or rather, because the work of art is indeed an object to which one can refer, cognitive denotation is not the mode of relationship to the object that captures its aesthetic interest. To describe an art object is not yet to grasp what makes it an artistic configuration. This is accessible only through an interpretation and evaluation in terms of the ambitions intrinsic to the object. There can be no neutral description of an artistic or aesthetic phenomenon. The selection of one work or phenomenon among others already expresses the conviction that it is a significant object, characteristic at least, if only in its qualities or failings. As for the description itself, it either reports on the object independently of all aesthetic considerations (in which case, why not the weight or the smell of a painting or book?), or it describes the object in terms considered aesthetically relevant and so on, on the basis of a choice guided by criteria of relevance.

A description is not neutral in terms of either evaluation or interpretation. The 'data' of a work of art are not 'given': like every signifying or symbolic object, it cannot be described without a hermeneutic choice—a choice evidently discussible but unavoidable—regarding the elements that contribute to the construction of a relevant account, the relationship

---

86 See ibid., ss. 57, pp. 211–14.

between these elements, internal relationships of correspondence or transformation, accentuations and focalizations, references and allusions, etc. An interpretative description of internal relationships must take account of the constitutive ambition of the work, of the meaning and quality of the relationships established, of the degree to which it has met its own demands, as well as the point and the relevance of these objectives themselves. This is why interpretation is indissociable from evaluation. The work of art is itself constructed in accordance with rationally justifiable criteria—even if the artist is incapable of articulating these discursively—that one can hardly hope to understand without reconstructing the *reasons* that account for its structure. That is to say that 'aesthetic pleasure' is only a very approximate description of what we experience when we engage with an artistic universe.[87]

From the point of view of the pragmatics of language, we do not then use the formula 'it's beautiful' to say 'this pleases me', but to claim that others, everyone even, should concur in our estimate. Unlike our preference for the taste of particular fruit, or the light at a certain time of day, it involves an evaluation based not on a merely private and admittedly personal pleasure but on reasons having to do with the qualities of the artistic object. Put more precisely, and limiting the scope of Kant's aesthetics, when we say 'this is beautiful' in the sense of 'this is a successful work,' we claim to make an impersonal judgement. When we say of a flower, a landscape, a person, that we find them beautiful, we find it easier to accept another's pointing out the idiosyncratic character of our estimate. Admittedly, just as we can prefer peonies to pansies, we can prefer Proust to Malraux, Greenaway to Wenders

---

87 Like perception, pleasure is irrefutable. This is not true of judgement based on such experience; to the extent that it includes a rational element, it claims to be shareable. Not being rational and liable also to be evoked by non-artistic objects, private pleasure cannot validate a work of art. See, however, Jean-Marie Schaeffer, 'L'oeuvre d'art et son évaluation' in Christian Deschamps, *Le beau aujourd'hui* (Paris: Éditions du Centre Pompidou, 1993), pp. 28–31.

or Bacon to Balthus. But to say that wallflowers are beautiful, or even that this one is particularly so, does not commit us to a great deal, given that the criteria in accordance with which we accord them this quality are to be found only in our own assessment or in a determinate cultural context. On the other hand, to say that a particular film, novel or painting is beautiful or particularly *successful* engages our judgement, in that we are responding to a claim by the artist that covers not just the qualities he favours—speed or slowness, lightness or seriousness, magnificence or asceticism—but the meaning and value of his artistic achievement, its success or failure. Looked at from a point of view that concedes nothing to magic or theological cosmology, a flower expects nothing from us (it is precisely this that makes it valuable for Kant). On the other hand, a work of art that is neither interpreted nor evaluated is dead; having no natural function, it depends entirely on the appreciation that gives it its life and can invoke reasons to justify its verdict. Unlike the judgement on a natural object, an aesthetic judgement of a work of art is necessarily warranted or unwarranted in that it answers to a rational demand itself constitutive of the object.

Although these reasons cannot be as rigorously binding as theoretical or ethical reasons—being notably incapable of forcing us to experience pleasure or to assent to the particular values embodied in the work—they can nonetheless justify the assertion that a work is or is not successful. I can in fact assent to such a judgement without myself liking the work in question or concurring with the vision of the world that it expresses. Such a judgement can only be formulated after the fact. Kant correctly states that no doctrinal principle as such can guarantee in advance the success of a work produced in accordance with its directives. There is no *recipe* for producing a masterpiece. This follows from the fact that the success of a work has less to do with the underlying idea than in the way in which it is embodied, less with knowledge than with know-how.

The reception of a work is inseparable from its success or failure. Our entire description of a work will be different if we consider it to have failed rather than to have succeeded, for, in the two cases, description will be guided by different principles in regard both to coherence and point; and this we must be capable of justifying. If there is a cognitive element inseparable from aesthetic pleasure, then our pleasure is conditioned by certain intellectual requirements. We experience aesthetic pleasure, or rather—in order to unambiguously distinguish it from agreeable affect or sensation, from any preference for subject or style—*artistic* pleasure, only when we think we have reasons for it. When these reasons are good, there is no need to suppose that these have to do with conformism, even if that can evidently never be excluded. Rather than defend an artistic product for bad reasons (for example, that it brings back a memory), better to content oneself with the experience of private pleasure, taking ones stance outside all aesthetic argument.

In his interesting article on the work of art and its evaluation, Jean-Marie Schaeffer writes: 'To deny that an object is a work of art in the evaluative sense of the term thus presupposes that it is one in the genetic, generic, semiotic, functional or institutional sense',[88] by this suggesting that the fact of being, for example, a text with ambitions to poetry, a human product, a symbolic structure, an object used for aesthetic ends among others, institutionally recognized, is enough to make an object a work of art even before it is submitted to any evaluation whatsoever. For Schaeffer, in other words, the concept of a work of art is logically independent of any aesthetic judgement, and this comes down to saying that, unlike the concept of the 'beautiful', that of the 'work of art' is a matter of determinant judgement in Kant's sense, not in the name of any aesthetic doctrine but quite simply in the sense of a factual or conventional determination.

---

88 Ibid., p. 22.

The reason why Schaeffer so relativizes the importance of evaluation in aesthetics is clearly stated in his book, *Art of the Modern Age*; he is opposed to the Romantic confusion between the 'cognitive discourse on the arts' and 'doctrine' in the Kantian sense of the term. 'In fact,' he writes,

> the speculative theory of Art treats art as a specific ontic domain *by virtue of its value*: it bases an ontology on an evaluative category. It confuses art as a phenomenal object with art as value; it defines it by its value and then valorizes it in return by means of its definition. Hence its distinction between art and non-art is inevitably a dividing line drawn within artistic practices: the act of exclusion is the complement of the sacralization.[89]

In his concern to oppose a secular dogmatism, Schaeffer wishes to exclude from the definition of art not only the implicit, a priori evaluation of the Romantics but any notion of evaluation whatsoever, even explicit, procedural and argued. It remains to be seen how an object, a signifying structure, etc., could attain to the descriptive status of a work of art without undergoing an evaluation that confers the title followed by an appreciation that assesses its relevance, something that cannot be left to private pleasure.[90]

The descriptive conditions that Schaeffer invokes are hardly sufficient. The argument is in fact circular; implicitly depending on prior evaluations or justifications, whereby a text aspiring to poetry, an artefact, a symbolic structure, etc., has been judged worthy of being considered as a work of art. The result is paradoxical: if the definition of art is inde-

---

89 Schaeffer, *Art of the Modern Age*, p. 64.

90 Ibid., p. 63: 'Neither does it [positive knowledge of the arts] preclude the possibility that objectal descriptions might motivate aesthetic judgments, it being understood that the traits described are chosen by virtue of the pleasure they elicit and not as traits defining the essence of the object in question.' Such a division between description and the judgement of pleasure comes down to the privatization of aesthetic judgement, robbing criticism of any possibility of intersubjective validity.

131

pendent of evaluation, one witnesses a positivist generalization of the Romantic a priori, in other words of an implicit judgement of value that distinguishes art objects from others.

Elsewhere, Schaeffer speaks of 'candidates for aesthetic appreciation'.[91] Now, to be a 'candidate for appreciation' *could* mean that the object is not yet 'recognized as a work of art'. Unless, obviously, one joins George Dickie in defining the work of art as 'an artifact . . . upon which some society or some sub-group of a society has conferred the status of candidate for appreciation'.[92] In this case, the trial by aesthetic experience is restricted to an 'appreciation' (like/do not like) *within* the category 'work of art', this status having already been conferred, the task of deciding what is art being left to the institutions.

There is thus an ambiguity in the term 'candidate for appreciation'. When Dickie employs it, he is thinking of works already recognized as such and it involves no decision as to the artistic character of the object. In 'appreciating' a painting by Vermeer or Rembrandt, in other words, in formulating my aesthetic judgement on the basis of my own irreplaceable experience, even should my judgement prove negative, there is little chance of its excluding a work from the domain of art or changing the prevailing opinion of an artist. It is otherwise for 'candidates' as yet unconfirmed, for here it is a question of judging the category to which the object belongs (document, useful object or work of art) and its possible artistic importance. In such a case, the fact of belonging to one of the descriptive categories that can be used to designate an object is not sufficient to qualify it as a 'work of art', and exclusion does not signify aesthetic recognition under other aspects (genetic, generic, functional, institutional,

---

91 Schaeffer, 'L'oeuvre d'art et son évaluation', p. 22.

92 George Dickie, 'Defining Art', *American Philosophical Quarterly* (6 July 1969), p. 254.

etc.), for an object may be *analogous* to a work of art under all these aspects without actually being one. It is precisely for this reason that Danto constructs his series of analogies between 'simple objects' and works of art.[93]

The question of candidacy for the status of work of art can be posed in two ways: either, in all ages, as a distinction between art and dilettantism, or, since the early twentieth century, as a distinction between the ordinary object and the artistic object. Even the readymade does not erase the distinction between the artist and the dilettante; from the point of view of an incorruptible criticism, any old object declared a work of art by no matter who, even when accepted by the representatives of an institution that has lost any idea of what it is doing, does not as a result acquire the character of a work of art worthy of the name.

This is why the 'claim' to be a work of art is not the same as an aeroplane's claim to be 'capable of flying'.[94] In fact, even an aeroplane incapable of flight retains its descriptive identity as an aeroplane. On the other hand, an object that is a candidate for the title of work of art that fulfils none of the minimum conditions demanded of a work of art (negatively: not to be a badly put together personal document[95]), that is not just 'not capable of flying' but also 'not an aeroplane'. The negative evaluation leads to its losing it descriptive character as a work of art. 'Who decides?' asks Schaeffer.[96] A prudent reply would be: the informed public as a whole, to the extent that the filtering institutions allow it the opportunity;

---

93 Danto, *The Transfiguration of the Commonplace.*

94 Schaeffer, 'L'oeuvre d'art et son évaluation', p. 24.

95 We shall see later how contemporary art has a tendency to rise to the challenge of the 'badly put together personal document'; but the fact that Richter or Boltanski have used family photographs doesn't make every family photo a work of art.

96 Schaeffer, 'L'oeuvre d'art et son évaluation', p. 23.

in any case, neither the creator alone, nor any *one* person, who relies on his own private experience to the exclusion of any criterion capable of being shared. In eliminating from aesthetics the apparently arbitrary character of all judgement (of exclusion or of quality), one fails to take account of the fact that we say of a person that s/he 'has good judgement' in matters of art, while others, who do not, recommend books, films, exhibitions and so on that aren't worth the effort, or present us with autobiographical, historical or quasi-scientific documents in which we find nothing artistic.

Nothing that lays claim to the title becomes automatically a work of art. Not everything prepared in the kitchen becomes a 'dish': what can one say of a chicken burnt to the point of inedibility, or a mayonnaise that refuses to take? All the ingredients are there, yet the 'work' is not convincing, all concerned concurring without difficulty in their evaluative judgements. It is not even certain that physical nature can be described without value-judgements.[97] The same goes, even more obviously, for works of art. One can debate the objectivity of judgements asserting that a work is more or less successful, but even a failed work must present certain minimal qualities to be considered a work of art. Having said this, there is no chemical test to show that one is faced with a work of art, and nor can Goodman's 'symptoms', which are something of this order, fulfil this function, because they are not specific to art. The refusal of the title of work of art must be motivated by criteria and by reasons.

---

[97] Theorists of science like Hilary Putnam have challenged this idea; see his 'Beyond the Fact/Value Dichotomy', *Crítica* 14/1 (1982), pp. 3–12; reprinted in Hilary Putnam, *Realism with a Human Face*, James Conant (ed.) (Cambridge, MA and London: Harvard University Press, 1990), pp. 135–41.

the question of criteria

Contemporary art has essentially abandoned the hope affecting political consciousness. Artists now know that social reality is little susceptible to their attacks on aesthetic expectations. What is more, whatever they do to find refuge in a non-commercializable, ephemeral or immaterial medium, the market and an arrivisme skilful in the use of techniques of reproduction have a long time ago transformed into 'aesthetic values' everything they have invented to sabotage the categories of traditional art; the 'sublime' itself has become an advertising concept. This is not an argument for a deliberately commercial art but rather for an art that has no illusions about the social context in which it intervenes, and which retains the possibility of offering a lucid response to it. Society has made its peace with contemporary art, opening its purse and admitting it to its temples. The subversion from which modern art derived its legitimacy perpetually risks neutralization by the welcome that it is offered. To assert its authenticity it has thus been obliged to seek other legitimations than that derived from its head-on opposition to society.

In this, there has been a great temptation to remobilize traditional aesthetic ideas, two of which have proved particularly appealing. As soon as it becomes difficult to know any longer what is properly avant-garde, one solution is to allow the pleasure of each to be the judge of what satisfies.[98] By radicalizing the Kantian Idea that there is no objective determination of the beautiful, one loses any criteria of shared, intersubjective evaluation, any 'normative' dimension to art.

Coming from another direction, one can avoid the question of aesthetic criteria through the idea of a meaning-effect that escapes the symbolic, rising above it or remaining beneath it, or even both at the same time: above in an *aura* constitutive of art in general, below in unconscious

---

98 Schaeffer, *Art of the Modern Age,* pp. 298ff.

effects.[99] The failing of such a quasi-ontological reading of art is to formulate a normative idea in demanding that an artwork worthy of the name produce a determinate symbolic effect, without specifying in what respect such an effect would be specifically aesthetic, and different, for example, from what is experienced in front of a tomb or an archaic cult object. A powerful tradition of thought, the phenomenology of aesthetic experience, is the site of a confusion of registers that make very different demands. With a metaphysical conception of the sacred—for which great art serves as the ultimate guarantee of the meaning and truth that seem to be directly revealed in it—is combined a philosophy of the body and of the flesh of the world and a perception of certain aesthetic qualities unjustifiably privileged. From the phenomenological point of view, the choice of the work considered seems to be self-evident: it is through an ontological dogmatism that the phenomenologist confronts us with the object of his/her choice and deciphers the meaning of its world.

Neither interpretation by pleasure nor that by normative signification enables us to escape the discretionary power of those who make the choices decisive for the perception of contemporary art. They do not help us answer the question put by Yves Michaud:

> How is it that certain efforts are seen not as work of the second or *n*th rank—been there, done that—but as amateur productions condemned to exclusion from the world of art? How is it that one can tell as easily as one does what is Art with a big A, and what is just popular art, or counterfeit, or lookalike—and that one can nonetheless as easily change ones mind, as witnessed by the cases of Combas, or Koons?[100]

---

99 Didi-Huberman, *Ce que nous voyons.*

100 Yves Michaud, *L'artiste et les commissaires* (Nîmes: Éditions Jaqueline Chambon, 1989), p. 36.

In matters of aesthetics, as we have seen, questions of evaluation are constitutive of the object itself. The descriptive approach presupposes an institutional decision that is implicitly authoritative. Yet faced with a concept of art radically destabilized by modern, avant-garde and contemporary works, one would like to have criteria that escape the idiosyncratic preferences such as are often validated by the institutions. By reason of the systematic intimidation practiced by the partisans of art since the avant-gardes reacted to the laughter of an uninformed public at the turn of the twentieth century, by reason of a false solidarity with contemporary art as a whole or with a galaxy of recognized 'names', and by reason of an evident lack of criteria, the essential distinctions are hardly ever any longer made. It is as if every experimental effort by a recognized name can now claim the status of an artwork in the fullest sense, as if any artistic claim in the name of radical experiment is more or less automatically part of the domain of art. It is not surprising that the rejection of contemporary art is sometimes just as undiscriminating. In the age of rules and well-defined artistic conventions, the difficulty was to create a work in defying them while in one way or another respecting 'the rules of art'. Today, faced with a complete absence of conventions, the difficulty is rather to create such rules. Together with the traditional rules, with the prohibitions, any notion of what is a valid work seems to have disappeared. One of the most lucid artists and theoreticians of contemporary art, Donald Judd observes: 'Quality, which is thought, breadth, intent, work, endurance and experience, all comprehensible matters, is nearly the definition of art.'[101] 'Comprehensible matters', that is to say, aspects of works that are analysable as symbolic realizations. These qualities there-

---

101 Judd, 'A long discussion not about master-pieces . . . : Part II', *Art in America* 72/9 (October 1984), p. 9.

fore have nothing to do with what Nelson Goodman, with his positivist distrust of value judgements and affective evaluations, excluded from his theory of symbols.[102] They are the specifically artistic aspects of the actual symbolic realization.

---

102 Goodman, *Ways of Worldmaking*, p. 66.

**aesthetic criteria:
criteria of exclusion**

According to Gerhard Richter, the absence of all criteria might be justified as a temporary necessity: 'Art is uncritically received . . . It hasn't always been this way, but at present it probably has to be—to avoid getting in the art's way, just for a time.'[103] He adds, however: 'I am sure that criteria will emerge, when we know once again what we need and what is right for us.'[104] One might see in this the reconstruction of the taste of an age. But when different people agree on what are the best and worst of his own paintings, 'then that confirms to me that we have an inborn ability to recognize quality and to understand painting.'[105] It is one thing then to reconstruct the criteria defining an historic taste, another to grasp more generally the functioning of aesthetic criteria which, for Richter, are

---

103 Gerhard Richter, 'Interview with Wolfgang Pehnt, 1984' in Hans-Ulrich Obrist (ed.), *The Daily Practice of Painting: Writings and Interviews 1962–1993*, trans. David Britt (London: Thames and Hudson, Anthony d'Offay Gallery, 1995), p. 118.

104 Ibid.

105 Ibid.

anchored in the powers of our reason. It is a question of this second type that will be tackled in this chapter, for the restoration of something like a shared taste based on absolute criteria seems both unlikely and undesirable.[106] Yet tolerance and openness to diversity are not a sufficient response to the inevitable problems of choice and priorities; they do not tell us what is a good aesthetic argument, nor do they exclude the existence, in this field, of arguments that are more convincing than others.

When one considers a work of art, it follows a principle that reveals itself to attentive examination, rules that allow one to grasp its ambition and measure its success. The hermeneutic destabilization that is especially crucial to modern works marks a break only with received opinion, not with all rationality as such, for otherwise art would escape all evaluation on the basis of communicable arguments. It is a fact, though, that we exchange arguments in attempting to persuade each other of the merits of this or that work of art. And contrary to Kant, in doing this we make reference to 'objectively' or rather intersubjectively analysable qualities of the works. It is true that these objective factors have meaning only in relation to imperceptible structures—such as the coherence of the whole, or the underlying idea, what Danto calls a 'theory'—concerned with both sensual and intellectual integration.

Such a coherence is not comparable to that of an argument about facts or norms; its logic is not that of truth or justice. A work of art—a *Garden Aeroplane Trap* by Ernst or a drip-painting by Pollock—can be 'incoherent' or even bizarre from the point of view of cognitive logic while being aesthetically coherent. It may display a coherence of humour, irony or derision, of tragic experience or epic temporality, of anxiety, melancholy or

---

106 See Yves Michaud, 'Des beaux-arts aux bas arts. La fin des absolus artistiques—et pourquoi ce n'est pas plus mal', *Esprit* (December 1993).

unease, of leisurely or jubilant rhythm, of monumental, hieratic, subtle or demystifying stylization, of broad or incisive gesture, of multiple techniques expressively coordinated. In everyday discourse, irony and anxiety, the tragic and the comic, each have their place but never succeed in constructing a world imbued throughout by such pervasive tonalities, forming a parallel universe distinct from everyday reality.

If the work of art is defined by the transformation of originally idiosyncratic experience into a symbolic coherence intelligible by virtue of its more than personal significance, then it is 'achieved' or 'successful' to the extent that it manifests such coherence. Achievement is measured by the discernible relationship between an intention and its realization. If a work of art can be criticized it is because it lays claim to a certain form of achievement. Whether it is 'careless' or deliberately unfinished, ruined, displeasing or formless, or an object removed from its usual utilitarian context—to be recognized as a work, one must be able to distinguish between an aesthetically motivated refusal of elaboration or completion and a state that is aesthetically indifferent or insignificant.

The risk run by certain tendencies in twentieth-century art, in attempting to aestheticize a priori everything in the world that could be thematized is, that if everything is aesthetic then one might equally say that nothing is and that in any event from this point of view, anything is as good as anything else. This being so, it is difficult to see why the 'works' of those, such as Ben, who take this position, should be given their place in a museum, rather than any other object; one might as well leave the world as it is and just look at it. If artists, galleries and museums feel it is right to exhibit them, it is because they consider, despite everything, that the signature affixed to these objects confers a new and unquotidian meaning on them; commercial interest alone cannot justify such exhibition. If we recognize the 'creator' as an artist, it is because we acknowledge, independently of the 'craft', a significant vision, idea or choice that reveals to us something that without them we would not have seen or thought. Even in the exhibition of 'any old thing', we are capable of discriminating between cynicism towards a public capable of swallowing anything and a 'poetry' that transfigures the real in incorporating it into a derealized universe. We are all the more prepared to accept such an application of coherence to 'any old thing' when the artist who invites us to follow him has already displayed a capacity for the transfiguration of the real, and we are in a position to recognize, in his innovations, a continuity in his own coherence.

The criterion of coherence proves inadequate, however, for establishing an order of artistic quality. Unlike the criterion of truth that suffices to define the cognitive status of an assertion, or the criterion of justice that serves to define the normative status of an action affecting the interests of others, aesthetic coherence is too weak. A true assertion offered as a solution to a problem does not need to be elegant or interesting as well in order to be appreciated as such; a just action or a well-founded normative judgement can be recognized for themselves without having to meet any other requirement. Consistency of stylization, on the other hand, is not enough to lay claim to artistic success.

Claims to truth or normative justice are situated in everyday contexts and accompanied by a commitment to justification. Art, whose operation suspends this everyday reality to provoke reflexive attention, has no anchorage of this kind. Neither the evaluations, expressions or the visions of the world that we articulate every day, explicitly or implicitly, are operations sufficient to constitute art. This requires that an aesthetic coherence that has become indissociable from its materialization in a work.

Truth, on the other hand, does not depend on the form in which it is stated, which can vary without affecting the force of the affirmation, no more than justice is subject to the character and context of application of the action or judgement, which may vary without putting the norms into question. As a result of its rupture with the pragmatic contexts of everyday life, art for its part does not dispose of a decisive criterion sufficient to define it. When ordinary reality is suspended and the reflexive attention of artistic activities has been established and the materialization effected, two criteria at least are added to the principle of coherence. This coherence must crystallize around an issue that is worthy of the demand for attention and gives complexity to the principle of homogeneity; and this constellation, once and for all crystallized in historical time, must meet the expectation of originality, contemporary relevance or 'novelty'.[107]

'It is considered undemocratic to say that someone's work is more developed or more broad in thought or more advanced, as complex as that term may be than someone else's.'[108] The juxtaposition of these three registers of appreciation in Judd is perhaps fortuitous, but there is here a necessity that more or less rigorously guides not only every aesthetic judgement but also the artist's own approach. For a work to stand up to its creator's own critical gaze, it must satisfy this type of demand.

Such criteria are not 'applied' from outside: they are simply registers that aesthetic judgement, if it is not to be heteronomous, can hardly avoid, but whose concrete implementation cannot be anticipated by theory. The

---

107 See Georg Lukács, *Philosophie de l'art (1912–1914)*, [= *Frühe Schriften zur Ästhetik* 1, *Heidelberger Philosophie der Kunst*], trans. Alain Pernet and Rainer Rochlitz (Paris: Éditions Klincksieck: 1981), p. 162: 'That "novelty" should be a necessary condition of art is the result of the coincidence in the aesthetic of value and its realization, of the fact that every work of art is the personal expression of its creator and cannot be separated from his personality, which is why every work must necessarily be distinct from all others; and because the creator produces as a historical personality, the "diversity" that he produces will not be an abstract alterity to other products but a concrete, positive expression of the historic moment: "novelty".'

108 Judd, 'A long discussion not about master-pieces . . . : Part I', *Art in America* 72/8 (September 1984), p. 10.

'achievedness' of a work of art is a notion as inevitable as it is seemingly subjective and relative. As soon as a theorist attempts to illustrate this idea by reference to a work, he enters the arena of criticism, which is no longer a question of aesthetic theory but of practical judgement. Here we are concerned to show only that the reception of a work of art is essentially effected by the recognition or denial of its 'achievedness'. The expectation of 'success', of the ability to 'stand up' under the competent, critical gaze, runs all the way through from the creation to the reception of the work of art. Without such a notion of 'achievedness', no understanding or even description of a work of art has a hope of being pertinent.

We expect a kind of 'necessity' of a work of art, and we are critical when we do not find it. It might be missing for a number of different reasons, and there are three reasons in particular for questioning a work's claim to the status of art: that it is *only personal*, that it is only testimony or documentation, or that it is *amateurish clumsiness* and *nothing else*. On the other hand, when we reproach a work for being only an exercise in virtuosity, we do not challenge its artistic credentials as such; we criticize it even though it qualifies as art. There is thus a distinction to be drawn between criteria of exclusion and criteria of merit. The three that we have just discussed are criteria of exclusion. 'Exclusion' itself is a concept that quite correctly makes us nervous, especially when associated with censorship or arbitrary judgement; yet it seems nonetheless to be analytically deducible from the very concept of art as making a claim to success. We must then distinguish between an authoritarian exclusion based only on arbitrary judgement or unjustifiable censorship by an institutional power, and an exclusion justified by valid reasons susceptible of being recognized by the candidate-artist himself.

In offering an example of two seemingly analogous usages, language helps bring out the operation of this requirement for achievedness. Thus a letter may be well-written while being neither art nor work. Its style may nonetheless produce an 'aesthetic effect', just as a flower, a chair, a train, a hat or a face can produce aesthetic effects or can be looked at from an aesthetic point of view. These effects are not necessary. A letter is still a letter, even if it does not produce them. The same is true of the flower, the chair, the train, the hat and the face; they too are still what they are, even if they produce no aesthetic effect. If one day I were to learn that a person who had been writing to me was 'in reality' an author who had hidden his identity, would his letters be thereby transformed into works of art? Not necessarily. But if this person then claims that these letters are in fact fragments of an epistolary novel only seemingly addressed to me, does that change everything? There is now indeed a 'claim to aesthetic validity', in the sense of 'aesthetic' not as a description of style but in denoting artistic ambition. Save exceptional cases, however, these letters will still retain a *private* character as opposed to the necessarily public character of the work of art, even when it reveals private details. The work of art has to be understood in itself, and not on the basis on contextual information; every ostensibly biographical fact is transformed by the intrinsic coherence of the artwork, should it be one. We expect art to manifest an intelligibility independent of any explanation by underlying motives. When a work is successful, a language thoroughly individualized attains to a power of universally intelligible symbolization.

The work of art thus has a public character. It is not merely evidence, documenting its creator—as would be a letter written for private ends— or it is that only to the extent that the creator's experience as embedded in it has in addition features that allow it to be understood in itself. In its coherence, the work transforms into an independently intelligible symbol what would otherwise be only a personal communication. When the work is successful, an individual structure, a 'private' language, becomes intelligible to a potentially universal public. One of the aspects of the artist's work is, precisely, on the one hand, to select those elements of personal experience capable of symbolic intelligibility and, on the other, to strip away that which has only personal significance, which lacks the ability to take on a sufficiently general significance. For we criticize those works that irritate us by being purely *private*. This first criterion thus leads us to distinguish between a photograph, a film or a narrative of purely private or personal interest and a work whose formal qualities present an interest independent of its creator, being intelligible even when one knows nothing of the creator and the sources to which he makes reference.

The second criterion leads us to distinguish between an object, a text, a film or whatever, that interests us by virtue of the *information* we may draw from it, from a work that interests us for its capacity both to compose a *vision* that pervades the whole and to lend itself to a multiplicity of interpretations. A letter by an artist or writer interests us for the clues it may provide to a better understanding of his work. But some of them can be 'minor literary masterpieces'. This may mean that their writer deploys, in relation to his addressee, a strategy whose subtlety or complexity are worthy of the plot of a novel. But this can also mean that, forgetting the addressee and in pursuit of no precise end, the writer has written a text that could equally well figure in a collection of his literary works.[109] In the first case, the strategically admirable letter is analogous to an aesthetically interesting advert, but it is not a work of art; in the second, the text is no longer specifically a letter: another reason we read authors' correspondence is that not everything in its is purely 'epistolary'. A painter might sketch on a paper tablecloth, pro-

---

109 See Lukács, *Philosophie de l'art*, p. 50: 'In a letter, for example, the possibility of objectivation, of producing an effect that goes beyond the mere personality, is purely fortuitous and is not founded in the very essence of the expression . . . For a letter . . . to quit the realm of purely personal communication, for it still to work for those to whom it is not addressed, who do not have the key to it . . . the letter must be inwardly finished and achieved . . . The fabric of allusions that forms the schema becomes a free, self-enclosed system capable of giving the impression, anywhere and everywhere, of being a complex of personal experiences.'

ducing a plan of the neighbourhood and indicating the way to his house. The sketch may unmistakeably display the characteristics of the artist's style: a thick, firm line; an elegant concision; a lively hatching filling in the blocks. Fetishistically devoted, we hang on to the drawing, which is an autograph document that has the same status as a handwritten letter of invitation from a well-known figure, but it is not a work of art. In the same way, should a composer whistle a few notes while out walking, would we be justified in turning on the tape-recorder? As a general rule, these letters, sketches and musical ejaculations have only documentary value.[110] The same goes for the swathes of texts or images whose function is to inform, solicit or engage, which, though they may be characterized by secondary aesthetic qualities and are intended to influence, or suggest for commercial, political or other ends, can hardly be considered to be works of art.

To read the Manhattan telephone directory,[111] the French Civil Code or Descartes's *Discourse on Method* as a work of art—and not simply to identify incidental aesthetic qualities—is the expression of personal whim, of disregard for the intrinsic ambition of the texts, or of an 'aesthetic' judgement of a non-artistic type. But such a reading does not account for the structuring intention of the work. Inversely, an advert whose aesthetic interest leads to the forgetting of the product that it is meant to sell is no longer an advert but an autonomous work whose aesthetic qualities outweigh its informational function.

---

110 See Walter Benjamin's 'Thirteen Theses against Snobs', part of 'One Way Street' in *Selected Works, 1913–1926*, VOL. 1, p. 459: 'A snob in the private office of art-criticism. On the left, a child's drawing; on the right, a fetish. Snob: "Picasso might as well pack it in!" . . . II. The artwork is only incidentally a document. No document is, as such, a work of art . . . IV. With artworks, artists learn their craft. With documents, a public is educated . . . VI. In the artwork, content and form are one: meaning [*Gehalt*]. In documents the subject matter is wholly dominant.'

111 Danto, *The Transfiguration of the Commonplace*, p. 136.

Genette draws an interesting distinction in this regard, distinguishing between an 'essentialist' and another, more open, 'conditionalist' conception of what make a work of art.[112] This distinction implies that one has to choose between a substantialist (or essentialist) perception of a work of art or a subjective perception of 'to each his own'. Genette, however, seeks to ensure the coexistence of the two criteria by defining 'essentialist literariness' by the formal criteria of fiction and diction: 'If a given epic, tragedy, sonnet or novel is a literary work, it is not by virtue of an aesthetic evaluation, even if there is universal consensus, but rather by virtue of some inherent feature, such as fictionality or poetic form.'[113] In fact, this 'feature' rests on a conception both 'conventionalist' (what deploys fiction and/or diction is considered to be art) and 'intentionalist' (what makes for a literary work is the author's intention to create one).[114]

At the same time, Genette limits the importance of intentionality: it doesn't cover the whole field of the aesthetic, in as much as there are works created without artistic intent that we nonetheless consider 'aesthetic'. For Genette, this perception is purely subjective: 'a page of Michelet or Démosthène is distinguished from a page by some other noted historian or orator only by some (in essence stylistic) "quality" that is a matter of free judgement on the reader's part and which nothing suggests was necessarily intended or even perceived by its author.'[115] The field of aesthetics is thus divided between essentially or constitutively aesthetic works in which evaluation plays no constitutive role, and conditionally aesthetic phenomena or texts the evaluation of which is purely subjective. Characteristic of this whole approach is the absence of any intersubjectively effective evaluation, or the

---

112 Genette, *Fiction and Diction*, pp. 4–5.

113 Ibid., p. 19.

114 Ibid., p. 28.

115 Ibid. [Translation modified.]

148

absence of an 'aesthetic logic' free of both subjectivism and objectivism. Such a logic is indispensable if one wants to avoid a definition of art that both admits 'botches' formally 'fictional' or 'poetic' but constructed without art, and allows attributions of artistic status that can hardly be shared, being based not on any aesthetic 'reason' but only on personal preference.

In the visual arts, conventions like those of fiction and diction can hardly any longer be identified, one of the reasons, perhaps, for the disorientation of criticism. But the Kantian question of 'how an aesthetic judgment can lay claim to necessity . . . How are judgments of taste possible?'[116] is posed equally in literature and in the visual arts. One finds in Goodman himself a distinction of Kantian inspiration, based on the opposition between determinant and reflective judgement. This involves the difference between two modes of symbolization, between denotation and exemplification:

> The fourth and final symptom of the aesthetic is the feature that distinguishes exemplificational from denotational systems and that combines with density to distinguish showing from saying. An experience is exemplificational in so far as concerned with properties exemplified or expressed—i.e., properties possessed and shown forth—by a symbol, not merely things a symbol denotes . . . Exemplification contrasts with denotation rather than with representation.[117]

What is shown forth, expressed or exemplified does not define an object conceptually, but calls up a predicate more or less clearly evoked; on the other hand, what is said, described, denoted, leaves no ambiguity as to the predicate in question. In the first case, a particular reality is in search of a universal concept that would designate it; in the second, a universal term

---

116 Kant, *Critique of Judgment*, ss. 36, p. 153.

117 Goodman, *Languages of Art*, pp. 253–4.

is applied to a particular thing, defining it. There is nothing of the aesthetic in designation or denotative definition; representation, on the contrary, may be aesthetic when it represents something as or through something else (e.g. Churchill as bulldog) thus employing a metaphor that suggests and shows rather than denoting.

The difference between 'cognitive logic' and 'aesthetic logic' can be illustrated by the problem of perception that confronts the viewer in the cinema.[118] Slipping into ones seat after arriving late for a screening of *King Kong* in the original version, and seeing the black and white images of a boat, waves, tropical islands, one cannot tell straightaway whether this is already the beginning of the film—itself produced by specialists in documentary—or a documentary about travels in Polynesia. One then attempts to interpret the images. If what we are looking at is a documentary, we are to understand the information communicated, while the 'beauty' of the images is an incidental pleasure. The information here is discursive, denoting anthropological, cultural, botanical, geographical and other facts. At the very most, the director may suggest a coherence of an aesthetic type by incorporating this information into a personal travelogue studded with anecdotes;[119] this does not automatically make the film a work of art in the strict sense of the term. In documentary, the different sequences are much more independent than in the case of fiction. If it is *King Kong,* on the other hand, the elements constitute a more rigorous unity, a beginning and an end more pregnant with meaning, a narrative or metaphorical coherence that composes a total vision distinctive of the maker's artistic universe; the different elements are more strongly related to this unity than to a reality that has no interest in itself. 'Beauty' here has

---

[118] See my article, 'L'oeuvre de l'art et ses doubles', *Critique* 514 (March 1990), p. 190.

[119] The reportages of Jacques Cousteau and the documentaries of Frédéric Rossif are examples of the juxtaposition or even interpenetration of these two logics.

another meaning; it refers to the artistic success of the narrative, to the adequacy of the medium, to its capacity to move us intelligently through its coherent and suggestive metaphorical fabric. Aesthetic evaluation is here inseparable from cognitive comprehension; it is what makes sense of the elements in terms of the point of the work (its intention and the means of its realization). Each item of 'information' is relevant only in terms of the overall composition and its artistic ambition. The objection that may be put here, if the information does not succeed in building up a suggestive over-all vision, is to the *purely documentary* character of the work presented.

The product of artistic activity, presented to the public with a view to its being recognized as a work of art, runs the double risk of the private and the documentary. A publisher can reject what claims to be a novel, saying that it is no more than personal testimony without artistic development; a painting or a photograph can belong in the 'family album', being of no public interest. On the documentary side, a text may be 'ethnographic', an image 'touristic'. Things become more complicated, however, when what is in question is a sketch[120] or draft of a work of art that may or may not have been completed later, and that is thus a 'product of artistic activity'. Such products are halfway between document and work of art. They have their artistic meaning only in relation to the projected work.[121] Admittedly, whether good or bad, the product of artistic activity will always be literary, pictorial or musical, rather than culinary, technological or political. But to present certain characteristics of a work of fiction or poetry, of painting, sculpture or music, etc., does not by itself make a work of art. Other features are legitimately required by criticism, distinguishing the work of art from amateur efforts or from the stylistic effect introduced

---

120 See Lukàcs, *Philosophie de l'art*, p. 174.

121 Consider the use that Michael Fried makes of Courbet's sketches in his interpretations: *Courbet's Realism* (Chicago: University of Chicago Press, 1990), pp. 69ff., 218ff.

into non-artistic activities. Here we enter the specific domain of 'aesthetic rationality'. They concern those aspects that constitute the artistic character of a work of art, which are judged in the name of the internal requirements of the aesthetic sphere. In any event, the *purely* private and the *purely* documentary do not attain to the sphere of art.

In one sense, 'purely private' and 'purely documentary' are not so very different; in both cases, one is offered not a work but testimony or evidence (personal or impersonal as the case may be). The distinction does however express an opposition: the personal and the documentary fail by excess of subjectivity or excess of objectivity to constitutive a suggestive vision or a singularly coherent language. What is lacking in the one—a point of view, or a world—can be found in the other; but neither succeeds in creating an eloquent medium, a 'language for one' that can at the same time speak to all.

A third criterion leads us to differentiate between the *contingent* qualities of an object offered as a work of art—the effects of clumsiness or chance in the execution—and those qualities *intended* or at least consistently and meaningfully *appropriated* by the artist in the context of his project. It is this non-contingency—a tried and tested 'know-how' or address—that is for us the sign of 'talent'. To take a successful photograph is one thing, to be a photographer another, and it is no more conceivable for an innovative painter to win recognition on the strength of a single successful work. Talent is revealed by the fact that the artistic interest of the work derives not from chance but from a reiterated sense of theme or motif, point of view, lighting, appropriateness of materials, of many other factors that make for the unity and meaning of a work.

If the too purely private or documentary vision represents a failure to create an artistic or 'imaginative' universe, the absence of such know-how is a technical problem of artistic language. However fiercely certain avant-garde artists may have rejected the idea, we continue to distinguish between the 'ordinary person' and the artist, the latter being one who has both a way of seeing and thinking distinctively his own *and* an ability to *express* this vision in such a way that it is available to all.

Modern art, avant-garde art and contemporary art have accustomed us to the subversion of the well-polished sublimity of traditional art. Very often, artists have tried to convince us of the greater artistic interest of the industrial object, of the random, the worn, the thrown-away, the deliberately or accidentally destroyed. Yet although we are now capable of seeing unsuspected aesthetic qualities in all kinds of phenomena hitherto despised and neglected, we still do not really consider them to be works of art unless and until they are incorporated into an artistic project. Despite all claims to the contrary, the notion of a work of art remains tied to the name of an artist, such names being associated with highly distinctive and well-differentiated endeavours, with individuals' characteristic ways of working. We continue to distinguish between the 'bad painting' done by an artist for very specific aesthetic reasons, and incompetence pure and simple; between the person who could paint otherwise and the person who cannot; between voluntary and involuntary clumsiness. A writer who fails to master his own language, a composer who has no 'inward ear', a sculptor who cannot foresee the effects produced by his work: none of these have much chance of being recognized as artists. An artist is someone who has the technical skill and knowledge to bring about the desired effect, whether polished or deliberately clumsy or formless. The absence of such skill remains a criterion of exclusion in all those fields where technical mastery of an artistic language is called for. This is not the case when the artist presents or combines readymade objects or contents himself with specifying the object to be created by technicians. Here, the judgement of skill bears on the capacity to define a significant project in a given artistic context.

criteria of excellence

A coherence of vision that characterizes an ensemble of symbols both personally and suprapersonally effective, endowed with an expressive power that differentiates them from merely denotative symbols and evidencing a non-contingent know-how—these are some of the distinguishing features of art; it is today, in principle, the medium of a sovereignty without limits, capable of application to 'any' dimension of reality judged to be aesthetically eloquent. It is in the name of such an expectation of coherence that we express disappointment at a work whose coherence is only trivial, or borrowed from other logics, e.g. from a cognitive logic; it is this that leads us to criticize works whose incoherence is unintended or gratuitous; to protest when an artist does not take his formal or stylistic choices to their necessary conclusion, as, for example, when black humour gives way to an emollient sentimentality, or when a work exhibits several unintegrated styles as often in an artist's works of transition between different 'manners'.

If coherence of vision is the condition *sine qua non* of art—in whose name we exclude certain efforts from the sphere of art altogether—the other criteria are more than anything criteria of merit or relative importance. Once it has crossed the threshold of art in going beyond the personal and the documentary and in attaining the required level of technical skill, a work is judged in terms of a number of internal criteria. The question now is not whether one is dealing with a work of art or a failed attempt to create one, or even something else altogether (a scientific experiment, a reportage, a useful or decorative object, etc.) but rather the degree of success, merit or importance that one attributes to the work.

Coherence, traditionally designated by the concept of 'form' or 'unity', here appears in a new light. It is not of a logical order, but constitutes the articulable unity of a vision, a conception, a style, a system of literary or pictorial metaphors, an order of sounds or rhythms. Incoherence deliberately and meaningfully deployed, chosen for its expressive value, can be another type of coherence. The concept indeed does not designate any particular type of unity; it implies that it is not only composed of elements, but of all the elements (or at least of a significant number of them) that are presented to reflective perception. Nothing more than this is to be understood by it, but everything that may be incorporated must in principle bear a relationship to what presents itself as a work of art. A plurality of readings is possible because aesthetic coherence is a coherence of the work as *medium*, which in one way or another always escapes the critic's conceptual reconstruction, revealing different significations from different historical and individual points of view; it is this that gives a work its energy and inexhaustible character. There is no absolute necessity in a work of art;[122] other solutions are almost always imaginable. Any such solutions must nonetheless present a certain logic in relation to the whole.

Debate here may thus bear on the *artificial* or *facile* nature of the unity, or on the lack of necessity—*incoherence*.[123] A work of art may be incoherent because a new style, a new conception, is emerging in its creator, without yet coming to structure the whole of the work. The form may be unsuitable to the subject; the technique employed may clash with the genre (e.g. the overly theatrical direction of a film), etc. In such cases, one speaks of a flawed work: not a *total* failure as when no meaningful coherence at all is achieved but a *partial* failure, in so far as the work has elements of meaningful structure and merits worthy of aesthetic attention.

---

122 Adorno, *Aesthetic Theory*, p. 188: 'What is only and thoroughly coherent is not [aesthetically] coherent.' [Translation modified.]

123 '[X] himself formulates, almost innocently, the reproach that one can address to his book . . . His project thus lacks necessity . . . It lacks the mathematical rigour, the passion for logic, that would have made his book an accomplished work.' (Josyane Savigneau, in *Le Monde* of 3 September 1993, p. 23). It would be difficult to find an analogous remark in contemporary art criticism, which has essentially lost the notion of 'necessity'.

On such an assessment of coherence, the work is not excluded from the sphere of the aesthetic but admitted with reservations.

How productive is the coherence will depend on a second parameter, on what is at stake in it, in Judd's terms, its 'depth'. It is when it lacks point that the coherence becomes artificial or facile. A geometrical form, for example, is eminently 'coherent' by reason of its symmetry, unity and ideality, but—unless one were to say that geometry as such has qualities that are not merely 'aesthetic' but 'artistic'—there is too little at stake for us to accord it, without further ado, the title of art. When Neoplasticism or Minimal Art employ geometrical forms such as the square or the cube, such employment, in so far as it is of aesthetic interest, raises issues regarding both aesthetic form and experience—the utopia of a world reconstructed in terms of its pure elements or of an art restored to its intrinsic three-dimensionality. This art of reduction to the elementary resonates with all that it has renounced so as to construct rather than to represent.

In certain cases, as for example that of a narrative work telling of some personal or collective disaster, the issue can be such as to shatter all artistic form. One realizes then that the interest of the work, which may be real and considerable, lies not in its artistic qualities but in its documentary force. Many works have had a passing impact due only to public interest in the subject, whether from a kind of mass voyeurism or as a pretext for historical or political debate and so forth. The work may be flawed because the artist was not equal to his or her subject. It may rapidly age, in that the point or issue that it articulates becomes dated and loses its interest, because it does not bear the impress of re-actualizable artistic form. It can be intolerable for an excess of naturalism bare of formal coherence, for excess of personal idiosyncrasy.[124] Artistic symbolization is by definition opposed to somatization and the public display of symptoms. However destructured it might be, it always entails this degree of sublimation. A work may be criti-

156

cized for the content or object of its intention being too much or too little dissonant in relation to the construction, the means of its realization, it thus having no 'depth', for its being purely documentary or still too rawly devastating to be susceptible of artistic presentation. Isolated from its form or specific coherence, the 'content' becomes the object of specialist criticism, whether psychological or psychoanalytic, sociological or historical, thus running the risk of a 'documentary' reading.

Form is nothing if there is nothing to be formed. The unity of the work is insignificant if it has not been won against resistant forces whose presence is still felt. A harmony that reconciles nothing carries as little weight as a chaos that presents not the least trace of meaningful order or expressive intention. The cloudless idyll is as impotent as the display of a desolation without limits and without, therefore, any aesthetic distance; a technical coherence achieved without resistance by the material or the content is without interest. Having said this, however destructured it may be, a work of art will always refer to a coherence without which the chaotic itself has no meaning. This is true at the levels both of formal choices and of subjects. The 'subjective' point of the work stands as a counter-pole to pure coherence. In the coming together of intention and the means to its realization, the non-aesthetic criteria of truth or ethico-political engagement are subordinated to the central requirement of aesthetic coherence, without which the content of the work would degenerate into a message;

---

124 'The die-hard fans, those who issue a blank cheque to every work by [X], will say that it is a "film d'auteur," a personal view. Granted, the images are beautiful, some of them magnificent, and sometimes they make one think of our great painters. Granted . . . but the autism displayed over these hundred-and-ten minutes provokes more than a sense of discomfort—a real anger.' [Marie Laure Le Foulon in *Télérama*, 2279 (18–24 September 1993), p. 94.] Evidently film criticism, like literary criticism, still has benchmarks that are hardly any longer to be found in art criticism.

the subject that is tackled is not more important than the aesthetically significant force that it confers on the work: 'A gutter well painted is of greater value than a badly painted palace.'[125] On the other hand, art is never completely a stranger to extra-artistic concerns, which it articulates and explores in their aesthetic and signifying possibilities; it cannot arbitrarily set aside criteria of truth and justice while alluding to an identifiable extra-artistic reality. In suppressing this pole, the purism of an aesthetics of a 'modern beauty'[126] opposed to realism and to the truth-claims of the avant-gardes is incapable of accounting for a single significant work. Aesthetic immanence is a matter of structure, and does not exclude the 'heterogeneous' issues that give art its power to disturb conformity.

As a perception of an experienced coherence, aesthetic pleasure consists—amongst other things—in the fact that the symptoms and the scars left by experiences of non-achievement and disappointment become meaningful, attaining an objectivated intensity that allows them to be considered at a distance. Rather than somatizing frustration or failure, art subjects them to liberating symbolization. This is what brings together, in art, the subjective expression whose criteria are authenticity and representativity and the objectivating evaluation that endeavours to identify experiences that are exemplary in the given historical context. In the examination of dissonances given form in significant works of art and capable of validation by criticism, the therapeutic analysis of symptoms joins the aesthetic critique of cultural values.

The relative failure of a work may therefore be attributed to its insignificance (when formal harmony is achieved against no resistance,

---

125 Karl Kraus, cited in Adorno's *Aesthetic Theory*, p. 149.

126 See Rüdiger Bubner, 'De quelques conditions devant être remplies par une esthétique contemporaine' in Rainer Rochlitz (ed.), *Théories esthétiques après Adorno* (Arles: Actes Sud, 1990) and Ferry, *Homo Aestheticus*.

over no significant issue) or to excessive significance (when a documentary naturalism or an unspeakable suffering shatter aesthetic form).[127]

And finally—the last parameter—it is possible for a work, a painting, for example, to present both a coherent vision and a historically recon-structible point, important and formally elaborated, but fail to evoke in us the fascinated attention that we associate with aesthetic experience. It lacks the element of profound actuality that would touch us directly. Hence the requirement of what Judd calls 'novelty', the most contested aspect of modern art.

Less than a hypothesis or a norm, the work of art is indifferent to time; its validity is inseparable from its concrete incarnation.[128] It answers to an historical expectation, often by 'disappointing' it by its very novelty. The dis-sonance that underlies the form is that of a precise historical moment. Important works can be forgotten, until the advent of a new historical con-stellation rekindles their interest for a later age. What in certain historical contexts could have been a work of art is in others no more than a clever imitation. The virtuosity of a Rubens or a Vermeer does not suffice today to make a work of art. In every age, for every art, there exists a certain hori-zon of problems, at the formal as at the intellectual and existential levels, which can be considered to be the problems of a then-contemporary work of art. A work can age to the point of no longer being capable of re-actu-alization, not only by revealing its inconsequence as a work, whose only interest lay in its surface actuality, but also by proving to be closely tied to a particular historical experience. It may then be criticized for its non-actuality, appearing, even at its moment of creation, as evidence of a past

---

127 The 'documentary' accounts of the concentration camps of someone like Primo Levi are more effective, more authentic and more instructive than artistic attempts to evoke such sit-uations, in which fiction and stylization prove to be intolerably inappropriate.

128 See Lukàcs, *Philiosophie de l'art,* p. 159.

phase of the history of art; it can also be criticized for a false, superficial actuality that consists only in the resemblance of its subject or manner to those of authentically contemporary works.

The art historian presents the succession of works on the basis of their formal innovations. Even in Greek Antiquity, thought to be innocent of the modern demand for 'originality', Sophocles and then Euripides certainly introduced the 'new' as compared to Aeschylus, in the number of actors deployed and also in the nature of their vision. In the same way, one sees in painting the gradual conquest of linear perspective, followed by its abandonment in Post-Impressionism, or again the course towards abstraction, or flatness, or three-dimensionality, or the use of materials hitherto considered unworthy, etc. No work can any longer be considered important if it contents itself with re-doing what others have already done.

There is in art no rule universal in itself; each artist arrives at his own. The aesthetic 'rule' is thus defined by this interesting paradox of being valid for only one person, so apparently furnishing the sole counter-example to Wittgenstein's refutation of the possibility of 'private language'. What it represents, however, is not a private language, but a semiotic and semantic innovation that enters the common language, becoming available to all. But this absence of a rule in turn becomes a rule, an obligation to non-repetition without which the very transgression of the principle in serial reiteration would have no meaning.

This necessity for novelty has become a subject of controversy only since its dissociation from other criteria. A break with the accepted idea of art became the single concern of certain elements of the avant-garde. With this, it became possible to define art, following Adorno and Derrida, by its subversion of the familiarity and dogmatism of ordinary language.[129] For Jean-François Lyotard, the modernist utopia is gradually reduced to a minimal gesture, analogous to the negation of the sensible world in the Kantian sublime:[130]

> The task of having to bear witness to the indeterminate carries away, one after the other, the barriers set up by the writings of theorists and by the manifestos of painters themselves . . . Do we have to have stretchers so that the canvas is taut? No. What about colours? Malevitch's black square on white had already answered this question in 1915. Is an object necessary? Body art and happenings went about proving that it is not. A space, at least . . . ? . . . Daniel Buren's work testifies to the fact that even this is subject to doubt.[131]

There remains the question of what makes these reductions *artistic*. Is it truly that only art can 'bear witness to the indeterminate'? In Kant, the enthusiasm for the French Revolution of the peoples of Europe (the subject of another of Lyotard's works[132]) plays the same role. If it is a matter of unsettling the dogmatism of ordinary language, certain subversive attitudes encountered in everyday life, and without any connection to art—irony, black humour, a sense of the absurd—are capable of achieving the same end. One might conceivably describe them as quasi-aesthetic but hardly as art or 'works of art'.

What is striking in the phenomena generally invoked in support of this thesis is the reduction of the work of art that gave symbolic form to a vision to a gesture that it is supposed to embody, as it is executed, Art in

---

129 Menke, *The Sovereignty of Art*.

130 Jean-François Lyotard, 'The Sublime and the Avant-Garde' in *The Inhuman: Reflections on Time*, trans. Geoffrey Bennington and Rachel Bowlby (Cambridge: Polity Press, 1991), p. 103.

131 Ibid.

132 Jean-François Lyotard, *L'enthousiasme. La critique kantienne de l'histoire* (Paris: Éditions Galilée, 1988), pp. 114, 133; Lyotard, *The Inhuman*, p. 104.

general, without distinction of form or work. One might thus suspect that we are here concerned with a function more necessary to the philosophers who legitimate these endeavours than to art in its contemporary diversity. Lyotard excludes from art everything that is exhibited in museums and thus falls under the ban of 'culture' and 'its pleasure',[133] of the 'culture industry' as Adorno called it, all for him without interest for any art that matters. One might ask oneself, then, how this art—present in no public exhibition space and so reduced to the perception of a few or the rumour by which it is propagated—could ever prove itself. Escaping all possibility of verification by the majority, the judgement that recognizes in this the essential Art is no more than the decree of a handful of initiates.

It is therefore better to accept that art does not today escape the ambiguous influence of the public institutions, and that these are consequently under an obligation to submit their choices to debate and to critical assessment. If not all viewers are qualified to come to judgements of exclusion or excellence, it should nonetheless be possible to make available to them the criteria by which some works and not others are judged worthy of consideration. Just as we do not accord autocratic powers to present-day governments, but require them to justify themselves before public opinion, so is it difficult to accept that the artistic choices made today remain, as is so often the case, opaque to us, even as it is in our name that the institutions show what they do. It belongs to our rationality to insist that a work of art be recognized for its demonstrable merits and not simply ideological solidarity or even as a result of a confusion of roles and responsibilities as between artists, critics and institutions, even if such constellations are in fact inevitable.

---

133 Lyotard, *The Inhuman,* p. 104.

PART THREE } **politics**

institutions:
the hegemonic taste

It is not enough just to make explicit the aesthetic criteria that implicitly regulate the relationship to art in the context of a modern, largely desacralized society. These criteria are not just set at nought by positivist or metaphysical aesthetic theories, by the compensatory needs that art is asked to meet. Aesthetic judgement is also bypassed by the power of institutional legitimation. As Michaud writes,

> state patronage can only go, by definition, to 'high', to 'real' culture. If policy-makers, inspectorates, arts centre managements and public sector curators support one artist rather than another, this can only be on artistic grounds. The procedure is clearly circular: Lavier is selected because he is important, and he becomes important because he is selected: a typical case of self-realising prophecy.[1]

---

1 Yves Michaud, 'Art, politique, pouvoir' in Roger-Pol Droit (ed.), *L'art est-il une connaissance?* (Paris: Le Monde Éditions, 1993), p. 312.

This is only one of many examples of the neutralization of any judgement and any criteria that arises from an unprecedented institutional situation. Works of contemporary art either have or do not have certain qualities discernible by criticism; however that may be, they are also subject to very different considerations, in particular as the objects of institutional strategies.

Despite the undeniable power of consecration in the hands of institutions, there is nothing that says, in principle, that the 'importance' thus accorded to an artist is related to the aesthetic qualities of his or her work. Innumerable artists hailed as crucial at one moment then fall into neglect, their works relegated to the cellars. The social weight of an artist has but little relation to the aesthetic value of his or her work as this might be established by critical argument or by the depth of the influence it has on other artists. This is a reservation that must also be addressed to Dickie's institutional theory.[2]

Whether it takes account of it or not, aesthetic judgement always presupposes a historical context, not just of artistic production and criticism, of selection by mediators such as the publishers of literature, but also—in the visual arts just as in music and performance arts—of presentation, of the provision and management of dedicated spaces, and finally, of policies that define priorities in the field. Over the first three-quarters of the twentieth century, thinking about art and politics focused primarily on the possibility, or even the necessity, of producing political effects by means of art. It is at this level that today an undeclared war is being waged between rival interests. The notion of 'the congruence of the field of the aesthetic with the field of political economy',[3] which once inspired rebellion, has changed its mean-

---

2 George Dickie, *Art and the Aesthetic: An Institutional Analysis* (Ithaca and London: Cornell University Press, 1974). See also Dickie's 'Defining Art'.

3 Thierry de Duve, *Cousus de fil d'or. Beuys, Warhol, Klein, Duchamp* (Villeurbanne: Art Éditions, 1990), pp. 39, 46, 72, 78, 89.

ing, now being a motive for adaptation to the realities of the age. The heirs of the avant-gardes and the Bauhaus have rediscovered the virtues of the academy and of tradition. 'Every teacher,' says de Duve, 'knows from experience that talent exists and that creativity is a myth. This the academy saw much more clearly than did modernity';[4] and 'if there is one word that deserves rehabilitation, it is tradition. To confine it to the academic when Dada is in the museums is to condemn oneself to the infantile, avant-gardist vision of history that regrets or denounces the "recuperation" of the avant-gardes and values rupture for its own sake.'[5] This is to forget that a 'tradition' as discontinuous and unstable as that of the art of this century is incapable of offering the advantages expected of the concept, precisely those of continuity, consensus, of warrantable quality and an assurance of future validity. If the most wholehearted defenders of contemporary art have reconciled themselves to the institutions, it is because these cannot be circumvented by anyone who wants to play a role in the 'world of art'.

In the field of music, particularly demanding of resources in terms of personnel, electronic equipment and so on, Pierre Boulez very early took up the institutional challenge, devoting much of his life to infiltrating the 'subversive':

> It's a matter of introducing subversion into the institutions themselves, permeating and radically transforming their internal processes . . . To meet the real artistic challenge, you have to deal with everyday problems of organization, learn how to manage institutions from within, rather than protecting your subversive impulse while proudly keeping your hands clean.[6]

---

4 Thierry de Duve, *Faire école* (Paris: Les Presses du Réel, 1992), p. 30.

5 Ibid., p. 62.

6 Pierre Boulez, 'Imagination ou bureaucratie' [interview], *Inharmoniques* 6 (1990), p. 39.

In the field of the visual arts, the Centre Pompidou opened with a Marcel Duchamp exhibition, thus marking the reconciliation between the institution and an art that systematically derided it. But a further step has been taken since in the fusion between contemporary art and public institutions. It is no longer a question of accepting an awkward and uncooperative inheritance, but of managing and stimulating current production. As de Duve writes:

> It's a matter of luck whether the political decision responds to a real need at the right time. The École des Beaux Arts de la Ville de Paris that M. Jacques Chirac, Mayor of Paris, decided to establish in 1989, came at the right time to fill a gap in the education provision of the City of Paris and to met the challenge laid down to art teaching in this period of cultural crisis. I had the good fortune to be brought into the project at a very early stage.[7] . . .
>
> Paris needed a major public-sector art school, a school open to all, without the financial obstacles of the private sector . . . a school that would offer an effective preparation for the entrance examinations of the great schools of art and design of the Paris area, and which would take its place beside them in enthusiastic emulation. This was the mandate we received from the Mayor, the mandate we endeavoured to fulfil.[8]

The resources at the disposal of the institutions are limited. 'The influence of the public authorities on the market for contemporary art,' writes Raymonde Moulin, 'is much more to do with the aesthetic choices of public institutions than with the level of financial resources committed.'[9] More

---

7 de Duve, *Faire école,* p. 19.

8 Ibid., p. 225.

9 Raymonde Moulin, 'Le marché de l'art', *Raison présente* 107 (1993), p. 153.

recently, a more ambitious cultural policy gives reason to believe in the institutions' lasting reconciliation with an art produced by avant-gardes which for their part had hardly received such support and would even have refused it if offered.

> In Eighties France close relationships were established between the 'aesthetic welfare state' and business, in the hope of escaping the dilemma of artistic freedom and security, saving the artist both from central government control and from the jungle of the market. In fact, rather than the impossible resolution of a dilemma intrinsic to the condition of artists, one has seen a growing complexity in the relationship between the judgment-market, influenced by the institutions, and the price-market.[10]

On the one hand, post-War cultural policy promoted a confusion between public recognition and aesthetic value; on the other, contemporary art has lost the radical autonomy that characterized both an avant-garde art that received no public support and the political stance of artists who owed nothing to anyone. An institutional context that resembles pre-modern patronage, although organized along supposedly democratic lines, now provides the framework for the creation and appreciation of an art that inherits from modernity and the avant-gardes a jealous concern for its own autonomy and critical character. The political tenor and effect of contemporary art are thus also conditioned by this indispensable yet cramping framework.

The internal difficulties arising from the logic of rupture find themselves reinforced by this change in the relationship between art and institutions. In the early years of the century, things seemed clear: since the middle of the nineteenth century, innovative art had been made, if not

---

10 Ibid., p. 156.

against the institutions—academies, salons and museums—then certainly apart from them, in conditions such that artists like Van Gogh or Picasso's friend Casagemas indeed merited the description 'suicided by society' conferred and again embodied by Artaud. Despite the personal success of Matisse and Picasso, and then of a number of Surrealists, the relationship between artist and institution hardly changed at all until the Second World War, if one judges by the number of avant-garde works then appearing in the museums. The first Cubist experiments and Dada provocations were welcomed neither by the museum nor by any other type of institution; at most they may have received the irregular support of a few private collectors.

Things changed, in France as in other Western countries, with the advent of cultural policies such as that of André Malraux, then of the President who gave his name to the Centre Georges Pompidou, to be followed by a 'democratization' of large-scale contemporary culture. Modern and contemporary art is welcomed into public institutions with open arms, contemporary artistic production is encouraged with public monies and supported by educational endeavours.

The crisis that has weighed on the art market since the late eighties has made only a partial difference to the situation. The innovatory work of recognized artists continues with institutional support, while those who are still awaiting recognition continue to work without any safety net, without the help of the system of subsidy established in better days, without the monthly allowances paid by galleries to the recognized artists they represent. Subversive innovation has thus come to look as if it had recovered its earlier function—before the institutionalization of contemporary art—once again opening up the prospect of a new generation of artists ready to die of hunger. Indeed, just as the Welfare State in periods of crisis cuts levels of benefit, and appoints cheats, idlers and foreigners as scapegoats of its own shortcomings, bringing back the market liberalism and social exclusion that it was supposed to have gone beyond, so the art market rediscovers the savagery that the system of subsidy had led one to forget. And with nomadic or mobile exhibition spaces, apartments and disused warehouses or factories transformed into temporary galleries,[11] all this apparent improvisation and 'poverty' seemed to have revived the spirit of heroic marginality that had been lost. In fact, the margins of the art market, like those of the jobs market, are 'nurseries' for a system that reserves it monetary rewards and benefits in kind for those who have the patience, the resources and the talent to persist despite the difficulties. Nothing suggests that the integration of the avant-gardes is only a passing episode.

The incorporation of modern and contemporary art into official culture has a number of different functions; it can be viewed in terms of the new functions of culture as well as from the point of view of art itself (of artists and critics). In disarming a potential of contestation and integrating it into the national heritage, it confers on government both the prestige of the patron and an aura of democratic generosity, of an authority open to the most subversive of criticisms. By offering public commissions to contemporary artists, as Malraux did with theatre ceilings, the authorities—whatever their political coloration, as the case of Buren demonstrates—show that they are not behind the times. By supporting a few projects as spectacular as they are controversial, they furthermore distract attention from their inability to deal with the endemic economic crisis. By the same token, all culture becomes 'mass culture', or, at least in theory, 'available to all'.

From the point of view of art, Millet describes the change as follows: 'The art of the twentieth century . . . wanted to win its own distinctiveness

---

11 See the dossier on FIAC 1993 in *Art Press* 184 (October 1993), pp. 24–5.

by escaping from the museum. Then, in the second half of the century, society replied by broadening the scope of the museum, like a fisherman casting a wider net in order to be sure of catching fish.'[12] The reasons for this 'fishing' remain obscure. One might think that involves only a change in attitude to the market. In reality, the most important implications are those that concern the aesthetic status of the work of art and the institutional status of artists themselves.

As for the new status of the work, this has been analysed most notably by Bürger. In the post-avant-garde period 'the category of the work of art has been resurrected and . . . the approaches invented by the avant-garde in order to oppose art are employed for artistic ends.'[13] Bürger is not here concerned to denounce a betrayal but to recognize a reality: the historical avant-gardes' attack on the 'Institution of Art', in other words on the autonomy that in bourgeois society stripped art of any relevance to life, has failed. At the same time, and for the same reason, the subversive and anti-artistic works of the avant-gardes themselves acceded to the status of autonomous works and, in the age of the neo-avant-gardes, end up being created for the museum. The concept of a work of art has been expanded, extending now to anything that presents itself as such. Bürger concludes that 'The neo-avant-garde institutionalizes the *avant-garde as art,* and thus negates genuinely avant-gardist intentions.'[14]

With this, the institutional status of the artist also undergoes a transformation. According to Millet, 'The novel thing about our own age is that contemporaries, better informed and more tolerant, want to make more

---

12 Catherine Millet, *L'art contemporain en France* (Paris: Flammarion, 1987), p. 271.

13 Peter Bürger, *Theory of the Avant-Garde,* trans. Michael Shaw (Minneapolis: University of Minnesota Press, 1984), p. 57.

14 Ibid., p. 58.

and more public spaces available to artists. The picture of the accursed and marginal creator begins to fade, and "suicided by society" gives way to subsidized by society.'[15] In itself, the disappearance of the "suicided by society" would be a good thing. The misunderstanding of art by its contemporaries and the consequent sacrifice of the artist is a situation that no one can find desirable. Yet Millet fears that subsidized art may lose what is in fact the best thing about it: 'If in a museographical society everything is done to display, preserve and promote the work of an artist, what role can the latter assign to utopia?'[16]

In principle, nothing prevents utopia from existing in a museographical framework, provided that this is supported by a society that itself offers room for it. If the museum seems an obstacle to utopia, it is because it threatens the visceral opposition between art and an institution defined as duplicitous, motivated by non-aesthetic considerations, as it was conceived of by the avant-gardes. What threatens to disappear with open conflict between artist and institution is the ethic of the avant-garde artist and the artist's status as a beacon for the intellectuals, precisely as a 'suicide': what seems to be disappearing is the dream of a *radically* different world, a dream that deserves to evaporate only to the extent that it is realized. Though artists, or a good number of them in any case, can now survive thanks to subsidy and the multiplication of exhibition spaces, it is a fact that society is far from being the world one might dream of, and the need for utopia is still with us. On the other side, there is nothing today to prevent one conceiving a museum that makes room for utopia, not in the

---

15 Millet, *L'art contemporain,* p. 280. De Duve, for his part, speaks of an 'age when the social position of the artist is not that of the accursed poet but more and more that of a cultural social worker' (*Essais datés 1,* pp. 135ff., n. 15).

16 Ibid.

sense of a world where art would be part of everyday life, or even in which everyday life is such a total art that art itself becomes superfluous, but in the sense that the works presented would open up horizons extending beyond society as it exists, in the sense that society—in its exhibition spaces as elsewhere—would admit the necessity of its own transformation. The museum could be—as it is already in part—a locus of critique in the public realm. It is not then in this sense that utopia is excluded by the museum, provided that one admits that 'utopia' can mean something other than '*total* rupture with the world as it exists'.

The real problem represented by the institution lies elsewhere. First of all, by virtue of its policy of incorporation, it effectively acquires, more or less openly, a right of oversight over contemporary art, not only as regards its exhibition but also it production. As Millet says, 'The very great freedom that late-twentieth-century society offers its artists is a conditional liberty. The new generation . . . knows that if it insists on its modernity, it cannot assert this through gestures of rupture. It has thus become expert in the deployment of ambiguity.'[17] Ambiguity, because it has to obey two contradictory imperatives—that of its own creative project and that of the implicit norms imposed by institutions' own conceptions of contemporary art: 'Driven by the inflation of art prices, museums are buying earlier and earlier in artists' careers, and so ever more rapidly ratify the decisions of the market. This has the advantage, for the chosen, of speeding success, but the disadvantage, from the creative point of view, of bringing to bear the weight of a hegemonic taste.'[18]

There is of course no *one* institution but a multiplicity of agencies and relationships which in principle ought to allow the development of a plu-

---

17 Ibid., p. 280.

18 Ibid., p. 272.

rality of tastes and contradictory commitments. It is nonetheless true that something like a 'hegemonic taste' really does exist, in so far as those who have the power to choose, to decide what counts in their eyes, do in fact constitute a restricted circle, one that applies implicit norms constituted within an identifiable ideological horizon. Such historical crystallizations are inevitable; they normally retain a certain flexibility thanks to inter-institutional rivalries and the periodic renewal of curatorial staffs. But we are faced here, in any event, with one of the channels through which implicit aesthetic judgements are enforced by the power of consecration.

But institutions' power is exercised 'upstream', through the system of applications, committees, grants, scholarships and commissions that create subtle and powerful links between the artist and the institutional context.

> A threat of the last 15 years to the integrity of art and perhaps even a cause of its decline is the growing bureaucracy for grants and commissions, all governmental. This is a bureaucracy for art, therefore art is needed to justify the jobs, and almost any art will do. Some money goes to mediocre artsits, wasting the money, which is scarce for good artists, and subverting the activity. Most of the money goes to institutions as support for the arts, actually support for the institutions. The activities of the critic and the curator may need integrity but that can't be asked of the superfluos bureaucrat, whose identity and complacency are as full, round and flexibly unchangeable as a rubber ball.[19]

The artist today, if not content with a quasi-clandestinity, is highly dependent on these kinds of people, sometimes closely connected to the critics, if not ex-critics themselves, seduced by the power involved in managing exhibition spaces.

---

19 Judd, 'A long discussion not about master-pieces . . . : Part II', *Art in America* 72/9 (October 1984), p. 15.

> The pressure by institutions, and even by some individuals, to produce institutional art is enormous. They're starved for their reflection. At the least the US government should not be involved in grants and commissions. The government is too dangerous: individuals are a nuisance or a threat; the people are kept scared, poor and dependent.[20]

But the influence of institutions goes deeper still. As managers of the exhibition *space*, they have a right of oversight over what has become one of the chief means of expression of contemporary art, precisely and hardly coincidentally during the period of 'reconciliation'. Now art creation takes place in cooperation between the administrators of the space and the creators of space that artists have now become. The innovatory rupture with already consecrated art is thus effected under the aegis of the representatives of authority. Hence the risk of an empty radicalism or a new academicism; earlier, rupture was motivated by a concern to preserve the vital experience of art from 'alexandrine' degeneration (Greenberg). With the reduction of avant-garde art to extremes, the spiral of the strategy of frustration has reached its limit. Beyond lies only the repetition of gestures— the *mise en abyme* of the *mise en abyme*—which, *inside* the realm of art, have lost their meaning, no longer affording the viewer a vital experience, either aesthetically or politically. Referred to its own emptiness, the public becomes indifferent or aggressive. The reconciliation proves false.

generalized suspicion

In so far as the relationship between the artist and the museums has been reversed, radicalization now being managed and thus neutralized by both

---

20 Ibid.

the market and the public authorities, the public has the sense of being the dupe of contemporary art. In the eyes of the public, the artist, whom they did not understand in the first place, is no longer even on the same side, as an adversary of the authorities, but seems to be in league with the latter in discomfiting them. So it is that the public rebels and rediscovers its old hostility to modern art. *Les deux plateaux*, better known as 'Buren's columns', offers the most striking example of such a confusion of genres, but one might also think of the Louvre Pyramid or Toroni's decorations for the Castello di Rivoli. Without intending to impugn the artist's sincerity or integrity, Millet notes:

> At the time of his joint actions with Mosset, Parmentier and Toroni, Buren had offered a few lapidary statements of the kind 'Art is no longer justifiable', and 'Art is false, painting begins with Buren, Mosset, Parmentier and Toroni.' One can imagine, then, what he felt about the contents of the museums. As he struggled to bring the Palais-Royal project to completion, this iconoclastic spirit was long gone. Buren explained that his intervention would not destroy the architectural equilibrium of the site, but on the contrary, would do something to bring it out.[21]

This view was not entirely shared by the public. The issue here is not whether he was right or wrong, but the apparent complicity between the authorities and an art which had seen itself as their most intransigent adversary. As Millet adds later: 'The art which for three-quarters of a century had been seen as fundamentally rebellious revealed itself as entirely capable of adapting itself to the constraints of the public commission.'[22]

The reason is perhaps its instrumental character. At the time of his opposition to the museum, Buren employed his artistic resources in pub-

---

21 Millet, *L'art contemporain*, p. 271.

22 Ibid., p. 279.

lic interventions intended to change the perception of space; equally instrumentally, he then claimed to reveal the architectural equilibrium of a national monument. It is striking that the aesthetic interest of the work entitled *Les deux plateaux* has hardly been analysed; supporters and opponents have both focused on the artist's discourse and the political background to the project. What is in fact revealed in *Les deux plateaux*? And what was it that disturbed its opponents, before the work fused with the monument and ceased to be a topic of discussion? The artist's standard stripes emphasize the castrated character of the columns, traditional phallic support of political authority, while the imaginary non-horizontal planes of the 'plateaux' disappoint orderly, rectilinear expectations. Yet the architectural rhythms of the site are respected and effectively highlighted by contrast.

To the extent that the artist places himself at the service of such national monuments, symbols of the power against which the autonomy of art was directed, the ethic of revolt against an ignominious society finds itself deprived of some of its legitimacy. Such a work will then be justified—*if* it is in fact justified—only by its aesthetic qualities. Otherwise, it is merely a fraud. The institution cannot indefinitely support an official art, or just anything at all; this demands competence in the decision-makers, together with transparency and explicit criteria: 'The whole question is how long the citizenry will agree to pay for people to behave as if they do not exist.'[23] But to behave as if citizens existed isn't simple either. As Bourdieu has observed, and as Fried never tires of pointing out, modern art (and in this respect, contemporary art—unlike the work of those such

---

23 Michaud, *L'artiste et les commissaires,* p. 20. See also the same author's observations in his article 'Des beaux-arts aux bas arts' (1993).

as Koons, who unreservedly exploit all the resources of the spectacle—remains essentially modern) is defined by its refusal to meet public expectations, by an intransigent insistence on autonomy.

If the uninformed public is disoriented, professional criticism is in no better state, hardly having criteria any longer upon which to base its judgements, and thus contenting itself with describing what it sees, as if the interest of an object was something that then leapt to the eyes, or reporting the statements of the artists themselves, as if it was for them to define the significance of their own works, as if since Conceptual Art, or even since Duchamp, the distinction between making art and analysing it had been abolished.

But most worrying are the astonishing reversals of position. It is easy to understand Millet when she criticizes Buren for doing the opposite of what he argued for a few years ago. It is less easy to understand the changes in perspective undergone by certain critics of international renown, whose thinking changes with the intellectual fashions, testifying to a profound disorientation.

In an article of 1977, Buchloh criticized Judd for having misunderstood, because of his formalism, the historical significance of the work of Yves Klein:

> How can one appreciate Klein's blue paintings without considering along with them the totally corny monogold relief paintings? What can the attraction of the sponge-paintings be once they are discerned as decorative relics of a derivative post-surrealist painting-into-object attitude? How can one appreciate the anthropométries without considering their act of production? How can one admire somebody's art disregarding his mind—supposing they might not be an integral whole—when the artist in question

on the occasion of the vernissage of 'Époque Pneumatique' indulged himself with quasi-fascistic announcements . . . ?[24]

In 1992, Buchloh had changed his mind—as he had every right to do. He believed that he had earlier defended Judd, which was hardly the case; but more notably he had changed his position on Klein, and so radically as to be perplexing:

> What I found appalling in Klein, it seems, was the way in which he had adapted, without the slightest compunction, the new techniques of spectacular culture to deploy them in the service of his own neo-avant-garde project . . . Judd appeared to be the American neo-avant-garde artist par excellence. He seemed even to have gone beyond this, in such a way that an informed public could continue to believe in the validity of art as an autonomous project with its own rigorous ethical and aesthetic norms. I didn't understand, then, that it was the very baselessness of Klein's wrong-headed claims (to have invented the monochrome, for example), his reactionary spirit and his wholehearted devotion to spectacular culture, that made him in fact an authentic member of the neo-avant-garde, paving the way for both Warhol and Koons. By comparison, American Minimalists such as Stella or Serra, and Judd as well, who insisted on the absolute credibility of their exclusive competence as painters and sculptors and on the permanent validity of the privileged forms of special experience that their work was meant to generate, had definitively installed, to even greater ideological effect, the spectacular at the very heart of the aesthetic of autonomy (even as they installed their work in

---

24 Benjamin Buchloh, 'Formalism and Historicity: Changing Concepts in American and European Art Since 1945', trans. Barbara C. Flynn, in ed. Anne Rorimer, *Europe in the Seventies* (Chicago: Art Institute of Chicago, 1977), p. 91.

corporate headquarters and the mythical public spaces of government commissions).[25]

In opposing these two forms of neo-avant-garde, what Buchloh sees as different is the relationship explicitly established with the society of the spectacle. Despite his reactionary inclinations, Klein is re-evaluated because he was not duped, because he made conscious use of art's worldly context, while the artists who abstracted from it, who persevered in a classical idea of autonomy are now accused of 'playing the game' of the society of the spectacle. In his re-evaluation, Buchloh entirely ignores any question of aesthetic quality, focusing entirely on the degree of awareness of the spectacular context that seems to have become the central concern of one trend in contemporary art. To highlight the function of given media seems now to pass for the creation of art.

Such a reversal, entirely a matter of ideology critique, suggests that the meaning of works of art can be reduced to the ideological function that they may fulfil in the socio-political context in which they intervene. Yet this type of evaluation ignores what, in every work of art worthy of the name, is irreducible to its political stance, even if, as Judd argues, no work can escape the latter.[26] The public expression of a political position, or even political reflection on artistic media, however radical it may be, does not in itself amount to a work of art or a proper object for art criticism. If the works and acts of recent artists are evaluated in this way, in terms of the lucidity with which they perceive their own recuperation by the spec-

---

25 Buchloh, *Essais historiques*, pp. 8ff.

26 'I once had an argument with a curator over the cancellation of an artist's show that was mildly political. The curator said that the museum was not allowed by charter to show art that has "political" content. This eliminates all serious art.' Judd, 'A long discussion not about master-pieces . . . : Part II', *Art in America* 72/9 (October 1984), p. 9.

tacle, it is because no other criterion seems to have survived the disappearance of traditional aesthetics.

consequences of the institutional turn

For certain 'avant-garde' movements, the link between art and politics was so close that political goals in some way took the place of aesthetic. Summarizing the ideas of the Russians and of Brecht, Benjamin writes that 'the instant the criterion of authenticity ceases to be applicable to artistic production, the total function of art is reversed. Instead of being based on ritual, it begins to be based on another practice—politics.'[27] Thus the political aesthetics of the twenties and thirties knew very well what it wanted to get rid of—an aesthetics of taste based on the detached and contemplative appreciation of works of art—but was not especially concerned with how its practice, now 'political', was anything to do with art. In fact, being an artist went without saying for those who put their talents at the service of politics.

Of projects commonly cited as 'politicized art', many were the work of artists first committed to forms of 'art for art's sake', the politicization being often an attempt to confer a social function on an art that indeed had hardly end but itself, and which ends up constructing formal towers of Babel, whether in Cubism, Expressionism, Futurism or Suprematism. The sovereignty of the modern artist who, after Cubist collage and the ready-made, was able by a wave of a wand to transform into art everything that came to hand, and was, first of all, a sovereignty of *appropriation* or annexation. This absolute power of aestheticization was later expanded, becoming an imperative to transform the world itself to meet the requirements of art,

---

27 Benjamin, 'The Work of Art . . .', in *Illuminations,* p. 218.

the artist becoming a revolutionary in passing from appropriation to *intervention* in an unaesthetic world. In so far as the sole criterion to survive is correctness of political analysis, the fact of being 'politically correct' suffices to legitimate a work of art. It remains to be seen what justifies it artistically, as art and, in answering this question, the theorists of political art have hardly succeeded in going beyond the clichés of traditional aesthetics.

What the purely formal and the politically motivated avant-gardes had in common during the first half of the twentieth century was their externality to the institutions. For a few years the art of the Soviet Union offered a sole exception, until propagandistic goals ceased to be accompanied by formal innovations. Neither Dada nor Cubism, neither Raoul Hausmann nor Georg Grosz found takers in the museums, and were acquired only retrospectively at a time when, as a result of institutional changes, the avant-gardes had lost much of their subversive potential. The post-War neo-avant-gardes were different, in that they most often *worked directly* for public exhibition spaces and were sometimes even commissioned by them. Most politicized art since the sixties can hardly be said to draw its legitimacy from its opposition to the institutions.[28] And unlike the pre-War avant-gardes, and whatever the artist's intentions, it is as works of art that their productions are displayed by private or public institutions. The exceptions represented by a number of sixties and seventies artists, 'decollagists' like Villeglé, or the early Buren or Stanley Brown,[29] are the last heroes of a resistance to institutional integration from which nothing can today escape for long. Even the occasional backlashes against contemporary art will do nothing to change the attitude of the institutions which, since the initiatives of Malraux and of the founder of the Centre

---

28 See Bürger, *Theory of the Avant-Garde*, pp. 57–8.

29 Buchloh, 'Formalism and Historicity', pp. 92–3, 99–100, 95–6, respectively.

Georges Pompidou, have been essentially open to and hungry for the most subversive experiments. In other countries, private foundations play the same role as do municipal, regional and national institutions in France. Neo-avant-garde practitioners or theoreticians such as Buren and de Duve have been appointed to head art schools of a new type that endeavour to square the circle in creating anti-institutional institutions or 'rehabilitating tradition'[30] by continuing artistic practices that sought only to destroy it. This institutional situation is in the process of undermining the certainties of contemporary aesthetics and opening the gate to certain intellectual regressions. Rather than admit that art could be a space of exemplary experiences, even within public institutions, independent of any allegiance to official taste, some attempt to bring about a forced reconciliation between art and society, while others cultivate on ever-more invisible margins a kind of residual Leninism of artistic insubordination. If the works and acts of recent artists are often evaluated in terms of the lucidity with which they perceive their own recuperation by the spectacle, it is because no other criterion seems to have survived the collapse of traditional aesthetics and the inability to generate an aesthetic pleasure that avoids kitsch. Since autonomous aesthetic achievement—which does not in itself presuppose either political or intellectual regression—has fallen under ideological suspicion, the degree of 'political' awareness, defined vaguely and generally and without regard for relevance to any given context, seems to have taken the place of aesthetic pertinence. For some critics, often among the most demanding, the creation of a work of art has almost become a crime, since a 'politicized' theory denounced contemplation, the complaisance of any self-sufficient work, the acceptance of the rules of the game. For such criticism, autonomous art has become a frivo-

---

30 de Duve, *Faire école*, p. 62.

lous genre, ethically irresponsible. From the political interpretation of works of art, criticism has moved on to a systematic denunciation from which highly reductionist endeavours are spared. And the contemporary rejection of this kind of censure in the name of individual pleasure as an aesthetic criterion only confirms rather than refutes the logic: as if the only alternative to the use of the resources of the visual arts to raise political awareness was their complete privatization and the abandonment of all possibility of a shared judgement of value.

If one wants to act politically or to make known ones opinions, there are other ways to do it than by borrowing from the arsenal of art. In itself, politics isn't aesthetic at all, quite the contrary. There is no moral obligation intrinsic to art practices requiring that their political implications be laid bare. If one were to exclude from art all those works that present forms or experiences without concerning themselves with their own contexts or political implications, there would remain, as works of art worthy of the name, only a few relatively recent productions. In other times, such forms of art have enjoyed considerable authority, an authority that is today reviving.

Within the dynamic of artistic autonomy, 'politicization' in the strict sense could only emerge—as we have seen—following a number of distinct stages: the refusal of subordination to religious and political order, that is, the conquest of autonomy, generally situated around the mid-nineteenth century; the purist elaboration of a language proper to art; accession to a sovereignty that allows art to subordinate all of reality to its own logic, absorbing it through derealization or the aestheticization of the real, in Cubist collage, in the readymade, or by intervening in it. It is only then that politicization comes to lay siege to unaesthetic reality, with a programme for the transformation of the world in the name of aesthetic autonomy. Such a project could only emerge at a time when political action seemed like an urgent everyday necessity in social life itself. Conversely, a revolutionary work presented to a public without political interests falls flat. For its significance to be understood, the public must share some of the values and convictions of the artists.

This is shown by the work of the Soviet avant-gardes and the influence they had on the art of the sixties. According to Buchloh, Russian Constructivism moves from a formalist conception, inherited from Cubism, Futurism and Suprematism, to a 'quasi-scientific' approach,[31] to 'interaction with the spectator',[32] and then to a 'utopian radicalism in the formal sphere'[33] that becomes increasingly problematic, failing in its efforts to 'address the new audiences of industrialized urban society'.[34] Whence the idea of photomontage and finally—that approach still being too closely connected with the unique, non-reproducible work of art—to documentary photography, 'in order to reach the new mass audience'.[35] With the move to photography there disappeared the last vestiges of the Constructivism that was to show reality to be transformable. Says Buchloh:

> The attempt to create conditions of a simultaneous collective reception for the new audiences of the industrialized state would very soon end issue into the preparation of an arsenal of totalitarian, Stalinist propaganda in the Soviet Union. What is worse, it would deliver the aesthetics and technology of propaganda to the Italian Fascist and German Nazi regimes . . . and later . . . the ideological needs of American politics.[36]

31 Benjamin Buchloh, 'From Faktura to Factography', *October* 30 (Autumn 1984), p. 87.

32 Ibid., p. 90.

33 Ibid., p. 94.

34 Ibid.

35 Ibid., p. 98.

But this is still to grant to artistic media too unequivocal a political status; in John Heartfield, by a devastating irony, photomontage took on a significance opposed to all propaganda. It is not adequate to impute the totalitarian hijacking to the concern for 'simultaneous collective reception'. The question that should have been asked was: is art the appropriate means for passing unequivocal 'political' messages? A glance at Constructivist works predating Soviet photomontage, notably those by Rodchenko and Tatlin, is enough to show that formal revolution does not necessarily have anything to do with political revolution. To reject illusionism and to use primary colours separated by line is in no sense particular to politically revolutionary artists.

This paradoxical absence of relation between formal and political radicalism reappears in the sixties and seventies, another period of political ferment. This was the last attempt to rescue the ethic of artistic radicalism from its institutional 'compromise' at a time when this had already been broadly established. In the time of the Russian avant-gardes, a government first revolutionary and then cynically managerialist sought to engage its avant-garde artists in the service of its propaganda, in consequence of which they were gradually stripped of their autonomy. In the Western societies of recent decades, it is the proponents of an instrumentalist conception of art who have sought to invest the institutions of art. But a project begun in the name of emancipation came up against institutional imperatives to which it had largely to subordinate itself. It was this situation that completed the confusion of criteria and led to the emergence of generalized suspicion.

---

36 Ibid., p. 109.

**political strategies:
public character and political content**

The most important factor in the temptation to make use of the work of art for political ends is the fact that it presents itself in the form of publicly accessible symbols. The writer, artist or composer offers to a public as large as possible works most often prepared or developed in intense privacy and isolation. This paradox of the publication of the private, most flagrant in the fruit of collective labour that is the *auteur* film, also affects the political dimension that a work of art may have. The more unequivocal its political message, the less distinctively individual its specifically artistic characteristics. Conversely, the more the work develops its own formal and compositional universe, its own technique and materials, the less easy it is to find in it a clear political intent. The artistic medium lends itself neither to denunciation pure and simple nor to the recommendation, in the form of propaganda, of any political preference whatever. Every attempt of this kind threatens to backfire.

When, under the title *Oil Painting. Hommage à Marcel Brooodthaers*, Hans Haacke presents a portrait of a smiling Ronald Reagan, set in a gold frame and lit from above, the intention is clear, especially when one finds opposite, separated by a velvet rope and at the other end of a red carpet, an immense mural photograph showing demonstrators opposed to his nuclear policy.[37] But why is the irony so quickly exhausted, transformed into a tedious counter-cult of a film-character set against the background of a society of the spectacle? In his taste for monumental forms, the artist shows himself to be fascinated by the emblems of power, by Mobil Oil and Mercedes, the undisinterested patrons of art whose racist actions he is right to denounce. He correctly emphasizes that it is difficult to speak of a 'politically non-engaged art' and that 'any public statement, including of course any artistic statement, has . . . social consequences, and this goes too for those that do not firmly identify themselves as "engaged".'[38] But this classic argument suggests a synonymy between 'artistic statement', 'social consequences' and 'politically engaged art'. Employing a strategy of culpabilization developed in the inter-War years, it calls on every artist not only to anticipate the social consequences of his/her work but, in addition, and above all, to clearly articulate his/her political position. The fact that the work of art intervenes in the public realm is understood to require that there must remain no ambiguity about ones commitment. As a result, no doubt, of the institutionalization of contemporary art, the exhibition space is seen as a 'court of public opinion'.

Yet nothing guarantees the supposed identity between the public and the political. No artist can predict the social consequences of his/her work, and explicit 'politicization' is not necessarily the most effective method of securing the desired socio-political effect for it. The fact that every artist evidences a certain attitude, if not specifically political then at least socially

---

37 For a reproduction, see Brian Wallis (ed.), *Art after Modernism: Rethinking Representation* (New York: The New Museum of Contemporary Art, 1984), p. 135.

38 'Zur Soziologie der künstlerische Strategie. Ein Interview von Hans Haacke mit Stefan Römer', *Texte zur Kunst* 8 (December 1992), p. 52.

identifiable, does not mean that the *thematization* of this attitude is the most artistically rewarding option. On the contrary, a manifest political intention threatens to cloud the socio-political experience to which the work testifies and which underlies its specific force. Today's confusion between the two terms is the symptom of a kind of exasperation of the notion of political art, this being short-circuited by the greedy tolerance of the institutions. The development of institutional heteronomy depriving political position-taking of the legitimacy that it might have had when the artist had no safety-net and risked a fatal fall at every step, it must henceforth find its justification in a relevance that is both political and aesthetic.

aesthetic principles and the political

The adoption of political positions may also play a role in adding value to the work. The 'political' importance attributed to a work, can, in fact, confer on it a secondary value more easily accessible than its aesthetic quality. Faced with the standardized or idiosyncratic characteristics of a great many works of contemporary art, the ability to grant them political or social significance is any easy way of re-establishing the public value of the work of art, compensating for the difficulty of finding aesthetic interest in it. There results a curious gap between what works actually symbolize and the secondary meanings attributed to them by critics or by artists themselves. This has been particularly true since the sixties and seventies.

Judd carefully distinguishes between political and aesthetic principles, without for all that denying the political issues at stake. He wrote, on the one hand, in 1975, that 'art, dance, music and literature have to be considered as autonomous activities, and not as decorations upon political or social purposes. Only in China and Russia is it still 1935.'[39]

On the other hand, reacting to the exclusion of Haacke from an exhibition at the Guggenheim Museum in 1973, Judd wrote to the museum's director: 'You can't refuse to show one kind of art. Any political statement, either by declaration or by incorporation into a context, can be art. You renege on every kind of art when you refuse to show a kind that is political.'[40] He thus rejected both the decorative subordination of art to political imperatives and the exclusion of political position-taking, given that it 'could be art'.

There is often something artificial about the relationships established between certain works and the political concerns of the time. What each of the artists proposes, the art critic Germano Celant wrote of the work he marshalled under the label of 'Arte Povera', is 'a possible socio-cultural strategy in which revolutionary and gnoseological processes shatter the system of industrial dictatorship. Today, in fact, the daily context is a "stage" on which intellectuals, students and workers "act", uprooted and isolated, as yet without making any affective connection with reality.'[41]

Such an intention is hardly detectible in the works themselves. For Arte Povera, as for European art in general, opposition to American art seems to have been a powerful motive: it was a question of 'creating an alternative to the modular and standardized procedures of Minimal Art'.[42] If for Judd political position-taking is a possibility of art, for the Europeans of the six-

---

39 Donald Judd, 'Imperialism, Nationalism and Regionalism' in *Complete Writings 1959–1975* (Nova Scotia: The Press of the Nova Scotia College of Art and Design, 1975), p. 222.

40 Donald Judd, 'Complaints: Part II' in *Complete Writings 1959–1975*, p. 208.

41 Germano Celant, 'Azione Povera' in *Arte Povera, Art Povera*, trans. Paul Blanchard (Milan: Electa, 1985), p. 89. [Translator's misreading of last phrase corrected.]

42 Ann Hindry, 'Quelques questions à Germano Celant', *Artstudio* 13, special issue, *Regards sur l'Arte Povera* (Summer 1989), p. 34.

ties and seventies the 'formalism' of the Americans was unacceptable. Europe seemed bound to express a consciousness of history in its art:

> Impossible here for artists to vindicate the cube and the line, steel and Plexiglas, and even more so to celebrate great stormy skies, frozen desert wastes. Impossible for them to exalt the cultural specificity of TV and the media. Everything is entangled and mixed up . . . artifice and . . . nature. What remains is the experience of disorder and unexpected combination. What lasts is the sense of the ephemeral that haunts everywhere, thanks to these ruins and these remnants.[43]

In reality, rather than counterposing the Europeans' history to the Americans' ahistoricism of forms and materials, the Italians mobilized a primitive nature and a culture equally 'un-European': Zorio's canoe and javelin and Merz's igloo; the nature reconstituted by Penone from its worked forms; Kounellis's caged animals, plants and materials; Anselmo's granite, magnetic north and lettuce all introducing a confusion of bric-à-brac into the exhibition space; nomadic furniture as in Beuys's winter garden and menagerie. The neon political slogan from General Giap that glows on Merz's igloo transforms a military strategy into an insoluble artistic paradox with no possible application. The mirrors in which Pistoletto captures our voyeurism and Paolini's variations on classical motifs have little to do with the primitivism and 'poverty' of the other members of the group assembled by Celant. Only an abstraction can serve to identify a commonality between these disparate investigations: the affirmation of a *heteronomy* opposed to the 'autonomy' and conceptual pretensions of the Americans, seen as 'Protestant' and uncritical with regard to capitalist technology and economy.[44]

---

43 Germano Celant, 'Un art nodal' in *Arte Povera,* trans. A Machet (Villeurbanne: Art éditions, 1989) p. 29.

In France, the Supports/Surfaces movement, concerned like Minimalism to deconstruct the easel painting, decomposed it into its material components, the unstretched canvas and the stretcher here taking the place of the 'boxes' and 'slabs' of the Americans. Here too a radical political discourse was associated with art practice, Marcelin Pleynet, in the Althusserian heyday, playing the role of Germano Celant. But rather than the Italians' heteronomous primitivism of nature or culture or the Americans' exploration of industrial forms and materials, the dominant model in France posited an identification with craft production, with the labour of worker and peasant. As Bernard Ceysson put it:

> Materials and ways of working always refer to the canvas, to painting, showing that the introduction of new materials only displaces the questions raised by an art practice, without overcoming the contradictions. In the use made of materials by Supports/ Surfaces, these are not denatured by their subjection to a poetics. It is very far from the 'Romanticism' of Arte Povera, simultaneously primitivist and technophile in the tradition of the Futurists. The acceptance of their ageing—their development in accordance with their material natures—does not express, for example, an anguish at the passage of time, an anguish that Minimalism crystallizes in its preference for shiny, smooth, neutral materials assembled to produce simple volumes, primary structures, presented as calm blocks, installed here on Earth for eternity.[45]

Like Haacke and Judd, like Beuys, whether on account of their politics or the triviality of their materials, Supports/Surfaces came into conflict with the

---

44 Germano Celant, *Identité italienne: l'art en Italie depuis 1959* (Paris: Centre Georges Pompidou, Musée national d'art moderne, 1981).

45 Bernard Ceysson, 'Propos à développer, à partir de Supports/Surfaces, l'exposition accrochée . . .' in catalogue *Supports/Surfaces 1966–1974* (Saint-Étienne: Musée d'Art Moderne de Saint-Etienne, 1991), p. 24.

institutions: 'The members of Support(s)/Surface(s) challenge the cultural structures supposed to determine the conditions of production and reception of art, establishing painting as a commodity value. Outside the institutional framework, the works "deposited" in various places—beaches, forests, quarries . . . can develop their autonomy and specificity.'[46] In general, this conflict, characteristic of contemporary art in the process of its institutionalization, is played out within the institutions themselves; the attempt to outflank them explains in part the short life of the movement and the ensuing reintegration of the now separated artists into the institutional system.

the sixties turn

Despite their cultural rivalries, contemporary art movements thus exhibit a number of common features essentially associated not with their political positions but with the institutional changes that have taken place in the field of art since the Second World War:

> 1. The formal experimentation of the earlier avant-gardes is now pursued in a decisively non-revolutionary social context and with the support (even subsidy) of the institutions, both private and public, of a society based on the market economy and liberal democracy.

> 2. This institutional status creates a void in the legitimacy of the neo-avant-gardes, one filled by discourses of secondary political legitimation, first censured, then increasingly tolerated by the institutions.

> 3. Since the fifties, contemporary art has been characterized by a change of scale, inaugurated by Abstract

---

46 Introduction by Y. Aupetitallot, ibid., p. 15.

Expressionism, in which the artwork becomes a counterpart of the same size as the viewer, or even bigger. This art is no longer made to decorate the bourgeois interiors in which works by Picasso, Matisse, Kandinsky or Max Ernst still found their place. It is an art of public exhibition, and, inevitably, more and more an art of public commission, a monumental art that has its parallels with the art of power and display that predates bourgeois domesticity—the decoration of churches and palaces—but this time in the name of an 'autonomy' 'guaranteed' by the democratic State, its regions and municipalities, its great organizations and corporations. If 'installation, as a fully institutionalized practice, seems to be suffering an expansionist delusion, according to which convincingness is a function of the area they succeed in occupying,'[47] this is also because 'installation' has always been the very type of a 'subversive' art that could not exist without institutional support and which embodies the relationship of forces between the artist and the institution *within* the latter.

4. This change of scale goes along with a radical anti-illusionism that underlies the adoption of three-dimensionality as against the pictorial surface, which leads from the painting as object to 'environment' and 'installation'.

5. Whence a tension between ostensible impersonality and an equally marked personal idiosyncrasy, the contemporary artwork compensating for its quasi-industrial, primitivist or naturalist depersonalization with personal

---

47 Buchloh, *Gerhard Richter*, VOL. 2, *Essais*, p. 57.

> myth; the singularity of the artistic vision, vanished from
> purposely impersonal forms and materials, returns in the
> identificatory investment of the objects.

Contemporary art risks becoming aesthetically unintelligible, by virtue of either a formal language too standardized or signs which rather than attaining the status of symbols remain no more than personal or collective emblems. But contrary to the expectations of traditional aesthetics, which has never stopped demanding that contemporary art produce 'humanly significant symbols', there on the frontier of this unintelligibility one finds the most important concerns and issues of contemporary art.

As Fried said of Minimalism, in a remark that is equally true of most contemporary work, whether by Judd or Warhol, Kosuth or Beuys, Arte Povera or Supports/Surfaces, works of art 'must somehow confront the beholder—they must, one might almost say, be placed not just in his space but in his way.'[48] For Fried, this is a sign of 'theatricality', a negation of pictoriality that precisely did away with any 'object' pure and simple and thus with any stagey effect of theatre.

In his *Aesthetics,* Hegel defined the move or 'advance' from sculpture to painting in terms of the power of sublimation of the pictorial surface.[49] And in the art that succeeds Abstract Expressionism, the retreat from such sublimation is motivated by a new 'experience', one that the sculptor Tony

---

48 Michael Fried, 'Art and Objecthood' in *Art and Objecthood: Essays and Reviews* (Chicago and London: University of Chicago Press, 1998), pp. 15–16.

49 Georg Wilhelm Friedrich Hegel, *Hegel's Aesthetics: Lectures on Fine Art,* VOL. 2, trans. T. M. Knox (Oxford: Oxford University Press, 1975), pp. 797–8: 'In sculpture the god confronts our vision as mere object. But in painting, on the other hand, God appears in himself as a spiritual and living person who enters the church and gives to every individual the possibility of placing himself in spiritual community and reconciliation with him.'

Smith illustrated by a car journey along a highway in the course of construction, at night, with 'no lights or shoulder-markers, lines, railings, or anything at all except the dark pavement moving through the landscape of the flats'.[50] This was an aesthetic experience, but one which for him 'did something . . . that art had never done.' 'Its effect,' Smith continues, 'was to liberate me from many of the views I had about art. It seemed that there had been a reality there that had not had any expression in art,'[51] but which for the artist had the importance of an aesthetic experience of the highest order, worthy of being acknowledged as such. 'The experience on the road was something mapped out but not socially recognized. I thought to myself, it ought to be clear that's the end of art. Most painting looks pretty pictorial after that.'[52] The artist did not realize, however, that such an experience was made possible only by a particular state of the 'world of art'; it needed Abstract Expressionism, Rauschenberg, Johns and Stella to have explored previously unimaginable possibilities of aestheticization for a discovery such as Smith's to become possible, communicable and significant within the aesthetic realm; Duchamp's readymade, a mechanical subversion of the artistic cult-object rather than a fascinated exploration of the world of non-art, would not have been enough.

The three-dimensionality of the 'new works' that Judd discusses in 'Specific Objects'[53] is intended to confront us with such experiences at the boundary between art and a reality not 'socially recognized'. The artists of the sixties sought to communicate an experience that could be rendered

---

50 Tony Smith, cited in Fried, *Art and Objecthood*, p. 157, from Samuel Wagstaff, Jr., 'Talking to Tony Smith', *Artforum* 5 (December 1966), pp. 14–19.

51 Ibid., p. 158.

52 Ibid.

53 Donald Judd, 'Specific Objects' in *Complete Writings 1959–1975*, pp. 181–9.

in painting only through illusionistic representation, and this precisely was incapable of suggesting the non-art aspect that is essential to it and which confers its provocative character on the repetition of a module. It was this same conviction that had already led Klein to look for the actual imprint of the real, of body, fire and rain; that moved Beuys to experiment with the fat and felt associated with a personal myth; that drew Warhol to images from advertising and photographs from magazines; that drove Anselmo to move blocks of granite around within the exhibition space, and Penone to deconstruct the worked natural object to bring out the tree in its earlier wild state. It is a question in each case of transgressing the frontier of the aestheticizable and bringing into art a limit experience generated in contact with an anonymous material that has become of obsessive interest to the artist.

It is this same discovery of a new aesthetic territory, until then excluded as unworthy of art on account of its raw and uncultivated character, which creates the tension between anonymity and personal idiosyncrasy. In so far as these materials are foreign to the universe of art as traditionally conceived, it is their entry into the life of the *artist* that legitimates their place there: their contact with Klein or with Beuys in the course of decisive experiences, the age of twenty-two shared by Penone and the tree, the impress of the body and breath in terracotta that gives solid form to these vital expressions. In contrast, the anonymity of the American work testifies to a much firmer belief in the artist's power to transform modern industrial forms and materials into art, detaching them from their everyday, utilitarian functions; it might be too that the Americans were less nervous in the face of a technology demonized by certain European philosophers.

The Europeans' reaction to American art looks like a mixture of jealousy, chauvinism and a most often misdirected ideological critique.[54] The rejection of Minimal Art, dismissed in the name of existential or political concerns, only imperfectly disguises European indebtedness to its discoveries—its new vocabulary of three-dimensionality, its impersonal materials, and its way of occupying space, without frame or plinth to mark the boundary of art. And the idiosyncratic gesture and personal myth insisted on by Klein, Beuys, Fabro or Penone is precisely what the Minimalists had abandoned in breaking with the pathos of Abstract Expressionism and with everything personal and familiar; it is what was ironized too in Lichtenstein's *Brushstrokes*.

If the Europeans were right to oppose Minimal Art, it was not on the political grounds often put forward as they endeavoured to regain for European art the centrality it had enjoyed before the advent of Communism and Nazism, but for aesthetic reasons. For there is not *one* type of experience that is in itself of greater relevance to art than any other: there is no universal language of art. The 'universal value' or exemplary success of a work is always tied to a singular realization without which its coherence will not be a matter of art—of a vision and its analysable materialization—but rather of geometry or of conceptual logic. For example, what distinguishes Judd's boxes from comparable geometrical modules is their human scale

---

54 See Donald Judd, 'Ausstellungsleitungsstreit' in *Écrits 1965–1990*, trans. A. Perez (Paris: Daniel Lelong, 1991), p. 224: 'The Americans have never dominated Europe. It's a false problem. All countries are still turned in on themselves in matters of art, and they distrust what is done elsewhere; consequently, certain countries react by denouncing the supposed imposition of American art. This self-enclosure leads to mediocre art. Some North American artists, during a certain time, produced better work. This work was recognized, although inadequately . . . These artists [Pollock, Newman, Rothko, Still] got no support in the city where they lived, New York, and they were certainly not supported by the American government, as seems to be suggested. They were all poor, and most of them didn't live long enough to benefit from the new market for art. The work done in the United States has nothing to do with American imperialism.'

and their position in space, the materials and colours, the equivalence of solids, voids and transparencies, all these making them invented objects that have never before existed, and no use for anything except perhaps to intrigue a human viewer, who becomes aware of his own spatial reality, his own mass,[55] his morphological incapacity to recognize identical elements arranged in space as what they are.[56]

While some have discussed Minimal Art in terms of 'positivism',[57] others have believed it possible to rescue it from this by claiming for it an unconscious symbolism which, from beyond the tautological visibility of the forms—'what you see is what you see'—'looks at us'.[58] But neither the depthlessness of a Judd or a Carl Andre, nor the emphatic profundity of a Beuys who hopes to regenerate society with the theosophical energies of his art, are in themselves artistic qualities. What count are certain eloquent constellations that come to function as symbols capable of fixing themselves in memory.

More than any political message, what is important are the indirect effects of that which has found symbolization in forms and materials, that which derives from the work of the artist as such, rather than of the ideologue or political messenger that s/he might also be. Just as much as Beuys's *Homogeneous Infiltration for Grand Piano*, an expressionist image of

---

55 See Thierry de Duve, 'Performance ici et maintenant: l'art minimal, un plaidoyer pour un nouveau théâtre' in *Essais datés 1*, p. 201: 'When a visitor walks on a Carl Andre checkerborad, he walks on something that speaks of his own human condition, minimised, reduced to the sheer *a priori* that makes him a thing among things, but a thing that knows it: a being whose existence is a burden.'

56 Ibid., p. 181.

57 See Eric Valentin, 'Beuys: mélancolie saturnienne et arc-en-ciel', *Artstudio* 4, special issue *Joseph Beuys* (Spring 1987), p. 43.

58 Didi-Huberman, *Ce que nous voyons*.

art consigned to the military ambulance, Judd's stacks and Andre's grids and checkerboards are emblematic of an art that was able to innovate and so accede to the specific experience of its age only by breaking with painting and sculpture to bring us face to face—beyond the boxes of stretcher and plinth raised to the status of artworks—with the unsuspected, revelatory qualities of anonymous objects in space. Without recourse to any referential suggestion, as deployed by Beuys in his therapeutic substances or by Warhol in the melancholy and narcissism of a celebrity infinitely reproduced, the Minimalist work derives its coherence from what it eliminates.

The inaugural phase of Conceptual Art seems to abandon the last vestiges of illusionism in radicalizing the hiatus between conception and realization found in Minimalism: '1. The artist may construct the piece. 2. The piece may be fabricated. 3. The piece need not be built.'[59] But this text, displayed in an exhibition space or published in a catalogue, does not escape plasticity. Kosuth's *One and Three Tables* (1965) presents a form of genesis of Conceptual Art: to a photographic image of the table, a 'classical' representation, he juxtaposes the real table, a three-dimensional object exemplifying itself, and then a dictionary definition of a table that reduces the object to a linguistic 'concept' visually exemplified. Here is the 'change . . . from "appearance" to "conception".'[60] For Kosuth, 'works of art are analytic propositions.'[61] All that counts now is the idea, as defining what counts as art—as Judd says, 'If someone calls it art, it's art.' Naming seems to sum up artistic activity as such, stripped of inessentials. And

---

59 Lawrence Weiner, 'Statement of Intent' in Gerti Fietzek and Gregor Stemmrich (eds), *Having Been Said*: *Writings and Interviews of Lawrence Weiner 1968–2003* (Ostfildern: Hatje Cantz Publishers, 2004), p. 21.

60 Joseph Kosuth, 'Art After Philosophy', in Gabriele Guercio (ed.), *Art After Philosophy and After*: *Collected Writings 1966–1990* (Cambridge, MA and London: MIT Press, 1991), p. 18.

61 Ibid., p. 20.

indeed, works of art offer no 'information regarding matters of fact': they have no documentary function. But self-authorizing declarative definition is not enough to make a work of art. This is shown by the 'photostats' of dictionary definitions, with their own characteristic plastic qualities in which one recognizes Kosuth's 'style'. In a second phase of his work, he tried to give this essentially linguistic form a socio-political function by using billboards (*Text/Context*, 1979) to post reflections on text, reflections more or less abstract and hence relatively ineffective, mistakenly claiming that that 'understanding signification' offers a 'key to understanding the political life of this society'.[62] It is only later, in a third phase of his work, that Kosuth takes full account of the plastic aspects of his use of language for pictorial or architectural purposes (*Zero & Not*, 1986) in the service of his philosophical ambitions. But, apart from the use of writing, this aestheticizing practice no longer has much to do with the initial programme of Conceptual Art.

During the seventies, American Formalism lost the certainty that until then had followed from its sense of 'specificity'. For Greenberg, it was the pictorial surface that was the specificity of painting. For Stella and Judd, it was the three-dimensionality of the canvas, and then of the object. For Kosuth, it was the idea of the work per se. Critics like Rosalind Krauss have thought it possible to draw a parallel between the abandonment of illusionism for this focus on specificity and the linguistic turn in philosophy that rejected the inarticulate interiority of the mind in favour of a public meaning crystallized in language. What is central to these (Kosuth's) works, she wrote in 1975, is 'their insistence on the exteriority, the publicness of the space in which verification and meaning reside. They are, one would say, visualizations of a linguistic space that is fully

---

62 Joseph Kosuth, *Interviews 1969–1989*, ed. Charles Le Vine (Stuttgart: Patricia Schwarz, 1989), pp. 98 and 104.

non-psychological—the attempt to picture a world unmediated by the idea of a protocol language, a kind of necessary purging of the fantasy of privacy from his art.'[63]

The American art of this period shares the scientistic ideal of analytic philosophy. But *all* traditional art of quality has in fact a symbolic 'exteriority' that makes it legible without reference to its creator's psychology. Certain modern currents, such as the Bauhaus, Soviet revolutionary art or the American art of the sixties, have aspired to a plastic grammar that nullifies the artist's subjectivity. But this is only one of the exasperated forms of the search for artistic legitimacy that characterizes the art of the period. The phrase of Judd's, taken up again by Kosuth—'If someone calls it art, it's art'—does little to hide the difficulty: the self-certification of the artist who believes he can bypass the critical judgement of others leads to a criterial lacuna that Judd, in his important writings of the eighties, would himself attempt to fill. It was at this time that American art, much later than the European, tried to provide art with political legitimacy or personal myth. Alongside Haacke there appeared young artists such as Jenny Holzer and Barbara Kruger who threw themselves into a political activism based on a feminist sensitivity to everyday violence and discrimination, engaging in an identity politics that put into question the privileged position of art made by Western white males.[64] At the same time, video-makers—men for the most part, like Bill Viola and Gary Hill— pushed to an extreme the scrupulous and grandiloquent examination of the artist's own body. The biologist of a human life stripped of language, Viola draws on family photographs to peer as closely at possible at his own

---

63 Rosalind Krauss, 'Sense and Sensibility: Reflections on Post '60s Sculpture', *Artforum* 12/3 (November 1973), p. 48.

64 See Claude Gintz, 'Ailleurs et autrement', in *Ailleurs et autrement* (Nîmes: Éditions Jacqueline Chambon, 1993), pp. 73–96.

mortal body suspended between the death agony of his mother and the birth of his own child, while Hill (*Crux*) makes a Christian symbol of his own limbs as they move through forest leaves. Whether through the political emphasis of the LED displays or the narcissistic strain of a video image magnifying the artist's vulnerable body, recent American art has sought legitimacy in the experience of the mortal body and the subversion of the discourse of advertising and propaganda.

As the final consequence of the institutional integration of art, one sees the development of a subtle collaboration between artist and institution, mobilizing substantial resources to transform the museum into a self-destructive and self-denouncing space.[65] The violence of the denunciation is balanced by the generosity of the funding, the institution hoping to be commended for an open-mindedness that sometimes verges on masochism.

The German Pavilion at the Venice Biennale of 1993 illustrates the paradoxical nature of the current relationship between art and politics, between American and European art. Under the title *Germania* (1993),[66] the US-based Haacke, invited by the German curator, took advantage of the commission to deliver a monumental denunciation tailored to the site and occasion of the exhibition. Above the entrance, an enlarged replica of a Deutschmark dated 1990, the year of reunification, takes the place of the eagle of the Reich.[67] Recalling Hitler's visit to the Biennale of 1934, Haacke

---

65 Gintz talks of *in situ* practices 'whose institutional success would immediately reveal their perfect congruence with the new exhibition technologies, and which would go astray in search of the conquest of space by signature and the establishment of a total environment.' Ibid., p. 10.

66 For this see Pierre Bourdieu and Hans Haacke, *Free Exchange* (Stanford, CA: Stanford University Press, 1995), which has discussion at pp. 125ff. and illustrations at pp. 117–23. Haacke's explanatory text, published on the occasion of the exhibition, is entitled *Bodenlos*: literally 'ground-less', meaning bottomless, unfathomable, unbelievable or incredible.

67 Perhaps a reference to Habermas's essay on 'Deutschmark nationalism'.

then hangs at the top of the stairs a photograph of that sinister occasion, framed in black—the same ironic denunciation as earlier applied to the presidents of the United States. Within the thirties pavilion, whose marble floor had been broken up, visitors found themselves making their way across the shifting, unstable debris, which clattered horribly underfoot.

The ambiguity of this very characteristic work of Haacke's derives from its monumentality and from the institutional context from which it profits. Its monumentality is ambiguous in its deployment of the grandiloquent, propagandistic scale of the madness it denounces in taking over the space offered by the official organizers. And the institutional context denies the very message of the work; for what is this society—a heap of rubble—that offers commissions to artists by whom it knows it will be denounced, and which the artist himself knows expects only that? This society is not just—morally—a heap of rubble left by Hitler, but also—politically—a democracy, ambivalent as it may be, like every other democracy that has ever yet existed, that cannot do without a critical art, and which indeed subsidizes it. The weakness of the work is its inability to incorporate this ambiguity. The conclusion to be drawn from this installation goes far beyond the point intended by the artist himself, revealing a political message weakened by its association with a collusive commission even as it takes itself to be radically subversive. This ambiguous message provokes a reflection as melancholy as it is critical; and it is this, perhaps, that is today the only 'political' effect a work of art may hope to produce. But the sense of scandal that is intended so finds itself neutralized.

'When it succeeds,' says Robert Storr in an interview with Eleanor Heartney, 'committed art makes people unhappily aware that the deeper

---

68 Eleanor Heartney and Robert Storr, 'Rien n'arrive par l'art', *Art Press*, special issue, *L'histoire continue* (1992), p. 54.

causes of social problems . . . are not obvious.'[68] He distinguishes such an art from one that 'reduces politics to an illustration or a slogan': 'W. H. Auden was right: "Art makes nothing happen." But far from signifying that politics has no place in art, this means that here, as in every other domain of experience, art offers us the possibility of imagining and scrutinizing things on which, in a certain context, we have no grasp.'[69] This assessment, that makes contemporary political art a witness to impotence, is no doubt more lucid, in the present context, than the blind self-assurance of any denunciation that claims to be effective. Storr connects the pertinence of any 'commitment' to a high standard of reflection: 'Art is in no danger so long as standards of reflection is high.'[70] There are reasons to think that a political art that wishes to go on the offensive without losing this intellectual lucidity requires a higher degree of politicization of the context. It is on the basis of shared historical experience that political art is capable of having a more or less substantial impact. The historical experience of today is however characterized by an atomization and a resignation that lend little support to such artistic activisim.

'Anything that disturbs people's sense of complacency is political,' says Bruce Nauman,[71] an idea that seems to be shared by many contemporary artists. He speaks of the anger he feels, more especially at our 'capacity for cruelty'.[72] He wants to make 'an art that aggresses against the viewer . . . because that way people are forced to pay attention'.[73] He endeavours to

---

69 Ibid., p. 55.

70 Ibid., p. 56.

71 Bruce Nauman, interviewed in Kristina McKenna, 'Art Carny: Like a barker outside a funhouse, Bruce Nauman lures viewers into his challenging and disconcerting art', *Los Angeles Times* (27 January 1991), p. 84.

72 Ibid.

73 Ibid.

disturb them aesthetically through his lugubrious stagings of cut-off heads, grimacing faces on video screens, neon signs that subvert and unmask stereotyped language. Neon and TV screen—advertising media addressing themselves to the individual—are thus turned into means for the public articulation of private thoughts and feelings which in the ordinary way have no place in the world of advertising and stereotyped television series. It is a matter of inverting the operation of the media and in this sense a 'political' hijacking or subversion of these languages.

Haacke is more specifically political. He attacks monuments (the German Pavilion in Venice, built during the Nazi period) and symbols (the Deutschmark in place of the imperial eagle) that have precise political connotations, with photographic evidence in support. He reduces to ruins a marble floor, a symbol of the unsteady ground on which the new Germany hoped to establish a normality impossible to achieve given the unforgettable past. The political content is unambiguous and even, from an artistic point of view, somewhat laboured. Nauman's revolt is skin-thin and ambiguous, bringing with it no precise political denunciation but rather an anthropological pessimism, yet it is aesthetically more subtle and disturbing.

Very far from Haacke's massive spectacle, more specific than Nauman's malaise, Gerhard Richter's *18 October 1977* cycle intends no particular 'mobilization' and issues no call for vigilance. As in his first works based on photographs, Richter takes the readymade aspect of photography as the springboard for an 'objective' expressivity. The photographic document—intimate record or advertising image, family snapshot or scene-of-crime shot—becomes the emblem of a post-historic age. Extracted from the family album where a repressed history lies in sleep, *Uncle Rudi* (1965) stands there smiling in his double-breasted Wehrmacht greatcoat. To this, Richter counterposes fragments of an equally elegiac beauty: significant others, romantic landscapes with distant horizons, still lifes, colour samples arranged so as to suggest emerging forms, the power of a gestural painting freed from any object, imaginary spaces, images of glaciation, of incandescence, of geological strata, mirrors, grey monochromes. This elegy of modernity demystifies what remained utopian in Duchamp's devastating irony: *Ema,* Richter's reply to *Nude Descending a Staircase,* is the artist's wife, whose photographic representation breaches only the taboos of the avant-garde; similarly, in their elegance and matter-of-fact simplicity, the *4 Glass Panels* stands to the *Large Glass* of Duchamp's *Bride Stripped Bare* as Carl Andre's checkerboards to Tatlin's *Tower.*

In his series on the death in prison of members of the Baader-Meinhof group, Richter paints what seems to him have been the fate of a politics of emancipation that allows itself to be caught up in an escalating violence. Working from photographs of the prisoners found dead in their cells, the crowds attending the funerals, an arrest in the open street in the course of a police siege, a sardonic confrontation, the record-player used to hide a gun, an empty cell, an image of unknowing youth, Richter leaves the viewer free to reflect on the aporias of radical political activity, 10 years after the prisoners' bodies were released to their families.

Most of the works that emerged from the sixties turn exploit aesthetic qualities foreign to both traditional and modern art (from Impressionism to Surrealism and Abstract Expressionism). They prefer to situate art at the frontier with non-art, with depersonalized forms and materials or with personal idiosyncrasy, in both cases at the limit of the communicable—untilled lands open to aesthetic symbolization. The notion of achievement disappears; the aesthetic satisfactions available are of the order of appropriation, with the integration of the most aesthetically recalcitrant realities. To account for this, recourse has been had to the Kantian notion of the sublime,[74] as if the non-art aspect were assimilable to the overwhelming magnitude or violence of nature which for Kant reminds us of the moral greatness of our reason. But the aestheticization of the limits of experience, whether depersonalized or idiosyncratic, is not adequately explained in the terms of a theory which, like Adorno's, in the end assigns philosophical tasks to art. It is better to see contemporary art as evincing a new openness to excluded experience, as an extension of the subjective world to include that which had seemed irremediably heterogeneous.[75] Yet even this interpretation is no more capable of informing a discriminating judgement of works of art. So long as art is defined in terms of a general philosophical or social function, the innovation, implications and success of any individual work remain secondary to the common task of emancipation or critique. Like art in general, committed art has to be justified in terms of aesthetic criteria quite independent of its political effectiveness. And such criteria distinguish each particular work from the general trends or movements to which it belongs, whether motivated by a rejection of Modernism or by a cosy huddling-up under the banner of Contemporary Art.

---

74 See Adorno, *Aesthetic Theory*, pp. 252–5, and Lyotard, 'The Sublime and the Avant-Garde' in *The Inhuman*, pp. 89–107.

75 Albrecht Wellmer, 'Truth, Semblance, Reconciliation: Adorno's Aesthetic Redemption of Modernity' in *The Persistence of Modernity: Essays on Aesthetics, Ethics and Postmodernism*, trans. David Midgley (Cambridge, MA: MIT Press, 1991), pp. 102–05.

the demands of art

In the face of contemporary art, criticism and aesthetics find themselves fixed in emotionally charged attitudes that most often express broader judgements on the present age. The current situation of art and of the discourse about it can be understood only by a reflection unimpressed simply by the long and prestigious ancestry of certain well-established ideas. Neither the obstinate outdoing of earlier avant-gardes, nor a return to the traditions from which the latter broke, nor any kind of neutrality, will afford a way out, each of these options being marked by characteristic illusions.

The aesthetic logic that might perhaps offer an escape remains itself naive so long as it does not understand the indirect effects of the institutional contexts that today frame all creation, validation, perception and interpretation of works of art. The gradual 'reconciliation' between contemporary art and cultural institutions, based upon the equivocal common interest of incompatible imperatives, has changed from top to bottom the idea that artists can have of their own work and its space of presentation. In particular, the scale of contemporary art, its manner of occupying space and its veiled aggression—nostalgic for the privileges of traditional art—

are all linked to this new relationship to the institutional. Caught in a trap, the public finds itself playing gooseberry in a courtship between 'curators' and artists that disguises a conflict of aims: for the former, to show a benevolent tolerance for anti-institutional aggression, or indeed to expect or solicit it, and for the latter to show that one hasn't been taken in by the institution of art and that one retains an unconforming independence.

Unlike classical Modern Art, contemporary art—whatever the means it employs—is nearly always somewhat disappointing; nothing truly Luciferian is any longer possible in these well-charted spheres. This indeed is admitted by artists and critics, the idea being probably wrongfully generalized to the whole of modernity. Asked what he would think if 'someone were to fall on their knees and break into tears before one of his paintings,' Richter replied that, 'Unfortunately, painting can no longer produce such an effect.'[76] And de Duve: 'I am not prepared to say that a urinal is great art. It is significant art, highly significant of the state of our culture. We live in a century in which great art is simply no longer possible, and all the great artists of modernity, even Manet, made their art from the realization that it was so.'[77] Is this really true of Picasso, Matisse, Masson, Pollock or Bacon? In fact, critical reflection on 'the state of our culture', as inaugurated by Duchamp, only became general with the neo-avant-garde art that came after the Second World War, representing a major iconoclasm whose entry into the museum poses the aesthetic problems that are discussed today. The choice between sacred art and ready-made, between aura and total derision, between beauty and political instrumentalization, is perhaps the dead-end we have to escape from, if only to be able to understand the works themselves.

---

76 Gerhard Richter in *Gerhard Richter* catalogue, VOL. 2, p. 102. A similar observation is to be found in Hegel, almost two centuries earlier.

77 de Duve, *Résonances du readymade*, p. 279.

The idea of an aesthetic logic is an attempt to escape this dichotomy, whose 'all or nothing' choice between act of faith and deconstruction misses precisely what is specific to art. A work of art reveals itself only when viewed from the right distance—not from too close, with the naive empathy of a bird pecking at painted grapes, nor from too far, with the disenchanted triviality of the professional nobody's fool who has just identified the iconographic model, fantasy, false consciousness or religious symbolism that undergirds the work. Too near and too far both have their own interest, once a work of art has been identified as such and forms part of the history of art. The loving contemplation of a decontextualized detail and the detached theoretical overview each have their own explanatory contributions to make, but neither takes the work seriously as such, making use of it rather for their own purposes.

A work worthy of the name is usually at least as intelligent as the informed viewer. This is why, whatever the critic might think, a reconstructible relation between an intention and its realization is fundamental to its appreciation. The other lessons one might learn, the evidentiary value it might have, have in the end very little to say about art. Susceptible to reasoned appreciation as it must be, the work is nonetheless irreducible to the explicit intentions of its creator. Aesthetic rationality is not confined to the conscious decisions of artists. Criticism deals with what makes for the 'grace' of a work, beyond the concept or conceptions of the artist. Richter remarks, 'I am amazed at how much better chance is than I am,'[78] while Bacon saw himself as 'a medium for accident and chance'.[79] But both knew that this grace would have been inaccessible without construction. Nor can a work

---

[78] Richter, *Gerhard Richter* catalogue, VOL. 2, p. 102.

[79] Francis Bacon in David Sylvester, *Interviews with David Sylvester*, new and enlarged edition (London: Thames and Hudson, 1980), p. 140: one of many such remarks to be found throughout.

founded upon no conception at all of the contemporary situation of art find 'grace', or benefit from 'chance'. On the other hand, even the most deliberate non-art can have its 'grace', so that one can identify a readymade of Duchamp's among a thousand more lumpish objects:

> Despite the legend that has it that Duchamp selected randomly the objects he exhibited, or ensured that that they were as undistinguished as possible, the most commonplace, chosen without taste—either good or bad—we have, at the end of the day, a series of objects that share a house style, a formal relationship among themselves. In other words, there is the same aesthetic relationship between a bicycle-wheel on a stool and a bottle rack as there is between Renoir's *Moulin de la Galette* and his *Balançoire*.[80]

Independently of the 'subjective judgement' of any critic,[81] there are—as every artist knows, and as the history of art accepts, in its identification of key works—some works that are better than others. Unless 'subjective judgement' here means the judgement that any subject would come to share were s/he to be brought to an adequate perception of the work by convincing description and interpretation. As opposed to what obtains in matters of truth or justice, the existence of an effective consensus is of little account in matters of art: conflict of interpretations hardly puts the world in danger. Yet when we state that a work is beautiful, successful or important, we do not mean to say simply that we like it; our aesthetic judgement implicitly claims to be based on good grounds that we are prepared to explicate.

---

80 Daniel Buren, 'Repères', *VH 101* 5 (Spring 1971), p. 35, cited by Buchloh in his essay in *Gerhard Richter* catalogue, VOL. 2, p. 89.

81 de Duve, *Essais datés 1*, p. 136.

Theorists such as Adorno have argued that objectively superior works are identifiable not merely within the work of an individual artist, but in terms of the history of art. Bach and Mozart, for Adorno, had had to repress their own taste for dissonance.

> Only Beethoven dared to compose as he wanted: that, too, is part of his uniqueness. And it was, perhaps, the misfortune of the Romanticism which followed that it no longer faced the tension between the permitted and the intended: this is a position of *weakness*. Now they could only dream of what was allowed. Wagner.[82]

Such categorical judgements can always be challenged and revised: what judgement could ever be immune from revision? But this kind of argument is not improper, so long as the qualities of works of art are susceptible of intersubjective appreciation. Beethoven's freedom was gained in painting perhaps only with Picasso, and Duchamp already found himself paying the price for the ensuing absence of constraint.

Making the degree of political consciousness a criterion of quality, is perhaps, like the rigour of Neoplasticism or Minimalism, an attempt to rediscover a constraint binding upon all, but it entails no aesthetic obligation. As Richter says, from the fact that Duchamp stopped painting 'one cannot ever deduce an obligation to give up painting. To understand Duchamp like that, and base ones politics or criticism on it, is appalling ... It gets you nowhere, it's neither art nor politics, it's just dilettantism.'[83] The dilettantism of a political analysis based on art rather on political realities themselves and the principles in whose name they can be criti-

---

82 Theodor W. Adorno, *Beethoven: The Philosophy of Music,* ed. Rolf Tiedemann, trans. Edmund Jephcott (Cambridge: Polity Press, 1998), p. 26.

83 Richter in *Gerhard Richter* catalogue, VOL. 2, p. 99.

cized; and the dilettantism of an aesthetic analysis that in the end doesn't need works of art to denounce contemporary society, for these only confirm what it already knows. Anti-dilettantism in aesthetics can only take its stand on what in art constitutes the distinctive significance and value of the works, qualities subject to an aesthetic logic; what, in the satisfaction afforded by the works, is not purely idiosyncratic. The 'autonomy' of art does not mean bracketing-out the extra-artistic issues of shared historical experience, but the filtering, transformation and re-evaluation of such issues by the rules the artist imposes on him/herself; it is through their coherence that the maximum effectiveness of artistic language is achieved.

Closely associated with the perverse effects of the hegemonic taste imposed by institutional power, a criticism whose criteria are matters of political dilettantism or of log-rolling pure and simple is for contemporary artists no more than a form of anti-autonomy and one more obstacle on the hard road to public recognition. If the modern inheritance of artistic autonomy is not to simply be frittered away, they have to exercise cunning and to accumulate the references, real or otherwise, that will gain them credit with influential mediators. It is an approach that opens the doors to false values and to the triumph of the epigone.

Philosophical dilettantism has led young artists to seek salvation in posting or even enlarging theoretical texts, as if the theorist needed the help of artists to make their ideas known or understood. But what theory hardly ever provides is any consideration of the distinctive power of art, its utopian force. It's hardly any surprise that much of the public should turn back to the art of the past and to the pleasures offered by the culture industry. To recover that sovereignty without which there is no art worthy of the name, contemporary artists must not only stand up against the received ideas of the established symbolic powers, but also confront the political and philosophical claims put forward by certain theoreticians with their own experiences and reflections, and with the demands of art itself.

ADORNO, Theodor W. *Aesthetic Theory*, trans. Robert Hullot-Kentor, Minneapolis: University of Minnesota Press, 1997.

——. *Beethoven*: *The Philosophy of Music*, ed. Rolf Tiedemann, trans. Edmund Jephcott, Cambridge: Polity Press, 1998.

ARDENNE, Paul. Review of *L'Art sans compas* in *Art Press* 178 (March 1993).

BARTHES, Roland. *Camera Lucida*, trans. Richard Howard, London: Vintage, 1993.

BASELITZ, Georg. 'Interview avec Demosthène Davettas', *Art Press* 123 (March 1988).

——. 'Entretien avec Dieter Koepplin', *Art Press* 159 (June 1991).

BATAILLE, Georges. *Literature and Evil*, trans. Alastair Hamilton, London: Marion Boyars, 1973.

——. *The Accursed Share*: *An Essay on General Economy*, VOL. 1, trans. Robert Hurley, New York: Zone Books, 1991.

BATCHELOR, David. 'Art & Language. Ce que peindre veut dire', *Art Press* 185 (November 1993).

——. 'Art & Language: What Painting Means. Interviews with Michael Baldwin and Mel Ramsden', *Art Press* 185 (November 1993).

BELL, Daniel. *The Cultural Contradictions of Capitalism*, New York: Basic Books, 1976.

BENJAMIN, Walter. 'Paris Capital of the 19th Century', in *Selected Works, 1935–1938*, VOL. 3, trans. Howard Eiland, Cambridge, MA: Belknap/Harvard University Press, 2002.

BENJAMIN, Walter. *Gesammelte Schriften*, VOL. 1/2, Frankfurt am Main: Suhrkampf, 1974.

——. *The Origins of German Tragic Drama*, trans. John Osborne, London: New Left Books, 1977.

BENJAMIN, Walter. 'The Concept of Criticism in German Romanticism', in Marcus Bullock and Michael W. Jennings (eds), *Selected Writings, 1913–1926*, VOL. 1, trans. David Lachterman, Howard Eiland and Ian Balfour, Cambridge, MA: Harvard University Press, 1996.

——. 'The Work of Art in the Age of Mechanical Reproduction', in *Illuminations*, trans. Harry Zorn, London: Pimlico, 1999.

BOULEZ, Pierre. 'Imagination ou bureaucratie' [interview], *Inharmoniques* 6 (1990).

BOURDIEU, Pierre and Hans Haacke, *Free Exchange*, Stanford, CA: Stanford University Press, 1995.

BOURDIEU, Pierre. *The Rules of Art*, trans. Susan Emanuel, Cambridge: Polity Press, 1996.

BUBNER, Rüdiger. 'De quelques conditions devant être remplies par une esthétique contemporaine' in Rainer Rochlitz (ed.), *Théories esthétiques après Adorno*, Arles: Actes Sud, 1990.

BUCHLOH, Benjamin. 'Formalism and Historicity: Changing Concepts in American and European Art Since 1945', trans. Barbara C. Flynn, in ed. Anne Rorimer, *Europe in the Seventies*, Chicago: Art Institute of Chicago, 1977.

——. 'From Faktura to Factography', *October* 30 (Autumn 1984).

BUCHLOH, Benjamin. *Essais historiques II*, trans. C. Gintz, Villeurbanne: Art Édition, 1992.

——. *Theory of the Avant-Garde*, trans. Michael Shaw, Minneapolis: University of Minnesota Press, 1984.

BUCHLOH, Benjamin, essay in *Gerhard Richter* catalogue raisonné and exhibition catalogue, 3 VOLS (Bonn: Kunst-und Ausstellungshalle der Bundesrepublik Deutschland; Paris: Paris-musées, 1993; VOL. 2 (French version), *Essais*.

BÜRGER, Peter. 'L'autonomie de l'art dans l'histoire', trans. P. Mésonnier, in exhibition catalogue *Where?*, Musée d'art moderne de Saint-Étienne, 1992.

CELANT, Germano. *Identité italienne: l'art en Italie depuis 1959*, Paris: Centre Georges Pompidou, Musée national d'art moderne, 1981.

——. 'Azione Povera' in *Arte Povera, Art Povera*, trans. Paul Blanchard, Milan: Electa, 1985.

——. 'Un art nodal' in *Arte Povera*, trans. A Machet, Villeurbanne: Art éditions, 1989.

CÉNA, Olivier. 'Le blanc souci de rien', *Télérama*, special issue, *Art contemporain*: *le grand bazar* (October 1992).

CEYSSON, Bernard. 'Propos à développer, à partir de Supports/Surfaces, l'exposition accrochée . . .' in catalogue *Supports/Surfaces 1966–1974*, Saint-Étienne: Musée d'Art Moderne de Saint-Etienne, 1991.

DAMISCH, Hubert. *The Judgment of Paris*, Chicago: University of Chicago Press, 1996.

DANTO, Arthur C. *The Transfiguration of the Commonplace*: *A Philosophy of Art*, Cambridge, MA: Harvard University Press, 1981.

——. *The Philosophical Disenfranchisement of Art*, New York: Columbia University Press, 1986.

——. 'Four-and-twenty Blackboards: Drawing and Thinking in the Work of Joseph Beuys', *Times Literary Supplement* (17 December 1993).

DE DUVE, Thierry. 'Who's Afraid of Red, Yellow and Blue: Barnett Newman Between Modernism and Post-Modernism', *ArtForum* 22/1 (September 1983).

——. 'The Readymade and the Tube of Paint', *Artforum* 24/9 (May 1986).

——. *Essais datés 1, 1974–1986*, Paris: Éditions de la Différence, 1987.

——. *Au nom de l'art, Pour une archéologie de la modernité*, Paris: Éditions de Minuit, 1989.

——. *Résonances du readymade*: *Duchamp entre avant-garde et tradition*, Nîmes: Jacqueline Chambon, 1989.

——. *Cousus de fil d'or. Beuys, Warhol, Klein, Duchamp*, Villeurbanne: Art Éditions, 1990.

——. 'The Monochrome and the Blank Canvas' in Serge Guilbault (ed.), *Reconstructing Modernism*: *Art in New York, Paris, and Montreal 1945–1964*, Cambridge, MA: MIT Press, 1990.

——. *Faire école*, Paris: Les Presses du Réel, 1992.

——. 'Yves Klein or the Dead Dealer', *October* 49/3 (1989).

DELEUZE, Gilles. 'Literature and Life' in *Essays Critical and Clinical*, trans. Daniel W. Smith and Michael A. Greco, London: Verso, 1998.

DERRIDA, Jacques. 'Cartouches' in *The Truth in Painting*, trans. Geoff Bennington and Ian McLeod, Chicago: University of Chicago Press, 1987.

DEWEY, John. *Art as Experience*, New York: G. P. Putnam's Sons, 1980 [1934].

DICKIE, George. 'Defining Art', *American Philosophical Quarterly* (6 July 1969).

——. *Art and the Aesthetic*: *An Institutional Analysis*, Ithaca and London: Cornell University Press, 1974.

DIDEROT, Denis. *Oeuvres esthétiques*, Paris: Garnier, 1968.

DIDI-HUBERMAN, Georges. *Ce que nous voyons, ce qui nous regarde*, Paris: Éditions de Minuit, 1992.

——. *Confronting Images*, trans. John Goodman, University Park, PA: Penn State University Press, 2005.

DOMECQ, Jean-Phillippe. 'L'Art contemporain contre l'art moderne', *Esprit* 185 (October 1992).

——. 'La crise de l'art contemporain', *Esprit* (February 1992).

——. *Artistes sans art?*, Paris: Éditions Esprit, 1994.

EHRENZWEIG, Anton. *The Hidden Order of Art*, London: Weidenfeld & Nicholson, 1967.

FERRY, Luc. *Homo Aestheticus*: *The Invention of Taste in the Democratic Age*, trans. Robert de Loaiza, Chicago: University of Chicago Press, 1993.

FRANCBLIN, Catherine. 'La passion du réel', *Art Press*, special issue, *L'histoire continue* (1992).

FREUD, Sigmund. 'Jensen's "Gradiva" ', in James Strachey (ed.), *The Standard Edition of the Complete Psychological Works of Sigmund Freud*, VOL. 9, London: The Hogarth Press and the Institute of Psychoanalysis, 1959.

FRIED, Michael. *Courbet's Realism*, Chicago: University of Chicago Press, 1990.

——. 'Art and Objecthood' in *Art and Objecthood*: *Essays and Reviews*,Chicago and London: University of Chicago Press, 1998.

GENETTE, Gérard. *Fiction and Diction*, trans. Catherine Porter, Ithaca and London: Cornell University Press, 1993.

GINTZ, Claude. 'Ailleurs et autrement', in *Ailleurs et autrement*, Nîmes: Éditions Jacqueline Chambon, 1993.

GOODMAN, Nelson. *Ways of Worldmaking*, Hassocks: Harvester, 1978.

HAACKE, Hans. 'Zur Soziologie der künstlerische Strategie. Ein Interview von Hans Haacke mit Stefan Römer', *Texte zur Kunst* 8 (December 1992).

HABERMAS, Jürgen. *Knowledge and Human Interests*, trans. Jeremy J. Shapiro, London: Heinemann, 1972.

——. *The Philosophical Discourse of Modernity*, trans. Frederick Lawrence, Cambridge: Polity Press, 1987.

——. *The New Conservatism*: *Cultural Criticism and the Historians' Debate*, ed. and trans. Shierry Weber Nicholsen, Cambridge: Polity Press, 1989.

——. 'Modernity: An Unfinished Project' in Seyla Benhabib and Maurizio Passerin d'Entrèves (eds), *Habermas and the Unfinished Project of Modernity*, trans. Nicholas Walker, Cambridge, MA: MIT Press, 1997.

HEARTNEY, Eleanor and Robert Storr, 'Rien n'arrive par l'art', *Art Press*, special issue, *L'histoire continue* (1992).

HEGEL, Georg Wilhelm Friedrich. *Hegel's Aesthetics*: *Lectures on Fine Art*, VOL. 2, trans. T. M. Knox, Oxford: Oxford University Press, 1975.

HINDRY, Ann. 'Quelques questions à Germano Celant', *Artstudio* 13, special issue, *Regards sur l'Arte Povera* (Summer 1989).

JUDD, Donald. 'Imperialism, Nationalism and Regionalism' in *Complete Writings 1959–1975*, Nova Scotia: The Press of the Nova Scotia College of Art and Design, 1975.

——. 'A long discussion not about master-pieces but about why there are so few of them: Part I', *Art in America* 72/8 (September 1984).

——. 'A long discussion not about master-pieces but about why there are so few of them: Part II', *Art in America* 72/9 (October 1984).

——. 'Ausstellungsleitungsstreit' in *Écrits 1965–1990*, trans. A. Perez, Paris: Daniel Lelong, 1991.

KANT, Immanuel. *Critique of the Faculty of Judgment*, trans. Werner S. Pluhar, Indianapolis and Cambridge: Hackett Publishing Co., 1987.

——. *Critique of Judgment*, New York: Barnes and Noble, 2005.

KOSUTH, Joseph. *Interviews 1969–1989*, ed. Charles Le Vine, Stuttgart: Patricia Schwarz, 1989.

——. 'Art After Philosophy', in Gabriele Guercio (ed.), *Art After Philosophy and After: Collected Writings 1966–1990*, Cambridge, MA and London: MIT Press, 1991.

KUSPIT, Donald. 'Le moi archaïque de Georg Baselitz', *Art Press* 77 (January 1984).

LE BOT, Marc.'Pensée artistique et logique sérielle', *Esprit* 185 (October 1992).

LUKÁCS, Georg. *Philosophie de l'art (1912–1914)*, [= *Frühe Schriften zur Ästhetik 1, Heidelberger Philosophie der Kunst*], trans. Alain Pernet and Rainer Rochlitz, Paris: Éditions Klincksieck: 1981.

LYOTARD, Jean-François. *L'enthousiasme. La critique kantienne de l'histoire*, Paris: Éditions Galilée, 1988.

——. 'The Sublime and the Avant-Garde' in *The Inhuman: Reflections on Time*, trans. Geoffrey Bennington and Rachel Bowlby, Cambridge: Polity Press, 1991.

MAKARIUS, Michel. 'Au plaisir des oeuvres' in Roger-Paul Droit, *L'art est-il une connaissance?*, Paris: Le Monde éditions, 1993.

MARQUARD, Odo. 'Indicted and Unburdened Man in Eighteenth-Century Philosophy' in *Farewell to Matters of Principle: Philosophical Studies*, trans. Robert M. Wallace, Oxford: Oxford University Press, 1989.

MATISSE, Henri. *Oeuvres de Matisse*, Collections du Musée d'art moderne, Paris: Éditions du Centre Pompidou, 1979.

MENKE, Christoph. *The Sovereignty of Art*: *Aesthetic Negativity in Adorno and Derrida*, trans. Neil Solomon, Cambridge, MA and London: MIT Press, 1998.

MICHAUD, Yves. 'Art, politique, pouvoir' in Roger-Pol Droit (ed.), *L'art est-il une connaissance?*, Paris: Le Monde Éditions, 1993.

——. 'Des beaux-arts aux bas arts. La fin des absolus artistiques—et pourquoi ce n'est pas plus mal', *Esprit* (December 1993).

MICHAUD, Yves. *L'artiste et les commissaire,* Nîmes: Éditions Jaqueline Chambon, 1989.

MILLET, Catherine. *L'art contemporain en France*, Paris: Flammarion, 1987.

——. 'Ce n'est qu'un début, l'art continue', *Art Press*, special issue, *L'histoire continue* (1992).

MOULIN, Raymonde. 'Le marché de l'art', *Raison présente* 107 (1993).

NAUMAN, Bruce. Interview, in Kristina McKenna, 'Art Carny: Like a barker outside a funhouse, Bruce Nauman lures viewers into his challenging and disconcerting art', *Los Angeles Times* (27 January 1991).

PUTNAM, Hilary. 'Beyond the Fact/Value Dichotomy', *Crítica* 14/1 (1982); reprinted in James Conant (ed.), *Realism with a Human Face*, Cambridge, MA and London: Harvard University Press, 1990.

RICHTER, Gerhard. 'Interview with Wolfgang Pehnt, 1984' in Hans-Ulrich Obrist (ed.), *The Daily Practice of Painting*: *Writings and Interviews 1962–1993*, trans. David Britt, London: Thames and Hudson, Anthony d'Offay Gallery, 1995.

ROCHLITZ, Rainer. 'Langage pour un, langage pour tous', *Critique*, 488–489 (January–February 1988).

——. 'L'esthétique, l'individualisme et la tentation néoconservatrice', *Critique* 521 (October 1990).

——. 'L'oeuvre de l'art et ses doubles', *Critique* 514 (March 1990).

——. 'Esthétiques hédonistes', *Critique* 540 (May 1992).

——. 'Logique cognitive et logique esthétique' in *Les Cahiers du Musée national d'art moderne 41: Nelson Goodman et les langages de l'art* (Autumn 1992).

SAUSSURE, Ferdinand de. *Course in General Linguistics*, Charles Bally and Albert Sechehaye (eds), trans. Roy Harris. London: Duckworth, 1983.

SCHAEFFER, Jean-Marie. 'L'oeuvre d'art et son évaluation' in Christian Deschamps, *Le beau aujourd'hui*, Paris: Éditions du Centre Pompidou, 1993.

——. *Art of the Modern Age*: *Philosophy of Art from Kant to Heidegger*, trans. S. Randall, Princeton, NJ: Princeton University Press, 2000.

SEEL, Martin. *Die Kunst der Entzweiung: zum Begriff der ästhetischen Rationalitat*, Frankfurt am Main: Suhrkampf, 1985.

SHUSTERMAN, Richard. 'Form and Funk: The Aesthetic Challenge of Popular Art' in *Pragmatic Aesthetics: Living, Beauty, Rethinking Art*, Oxford: Basil Blackwell, 1992.

SYLVESTER, David. *Interviews with David Sylvester*, new and enlarged edition, London: Thames and Hudson, 1980.

VALENTIN, Eric. 'Beuys: mélancolie saturnienne et arc-en-ciel', *Artstudio* 4, special issue, *Joseph Beuys* (Spring 1987).

WAGSTAFF, Jr, Samuel. 'Talking to Tony Smith', *Artforum* 5 (December 1966).

WALLIS, Brian (ed.), *Art after Modernism: Rethinking Representation*, New York: The New Museum of Contemporary Art, 1984.

WEBER, Max. *Economy and Society: An Outline of Interpretive Sociology*, ed. Guenther Roth and Claus Wittich, Berkeley: University of California Press, 1978.

——. 'Religious Rejections of the World and their Directions' in H. H. Gerth and C. Wright Mills (eds), *From Max Weber: Essays in Sociology* (New York: Oxford University Press, 1958), cited in Jürgen Habermas, *The Theory of Communicative Action*, VOL. 1, *Reason and the Rationalization of Society*, trans. Thomas McCarthy, Cambridge: Polity Press, 1991.

WEINER, Lawrence. 'Statement of Intent' in Gerti Fietzek and Gregor Stemmrich (eds), *Having Been Said: Writings and Interviews of Lawrence Weiner 1968–2003*, Ostfildern: Hatje Cantz Publishers, 2004.

WELLMER, Albrecht. 'Truth, Semblance and Reconciliation', *Telos* 62 (1984/85).

——. 'Truth, Semblance, Reconciliation: Adorno's Aesthetic Redemption of Modernity' in *The Persistence of Modernity: Essays on Aesthetics, Ethics and Postmodernism*, trans. David Midgley, Cambridge, MA: MIT Press, 1991.

RAINER ROCHLITZ (1946–2002) was a philosopher, aesthetician and translator. He was in charge of research at the Centre National de la Recherche Scientifique (National Centre for Scientific Research), Director of Seminars at the Practical School of the High Studies in Social Sciences and at the European University of Philosophy. He contributed much to make known the writings of the young Georg Lukács, Walter Benjamin and Jürgen Habermas of whom he was one of the translators in France. He also translated the works of Adorno, Ricoeur and Levi-Strauss. He died prematurely after a struggle with cancer at the age of 56.

DAFYDD ROBERTS is a translator from French and German, mainly in the fields of art, architecture and cultural history. He has translated catalogues and guides for many French and German galleries and museums, and for the past decade has been principal translator into English for the Centre Georges Pompidou. His translations include books and essays by Chantal Béret, Didier Ottinger, Michel Serres, Gilles Deleuze and Michel Foucault. He lives in London.